I0160912

THE TRUTH BEHIND THE LORD'S DAY

By
Pedro M. Prestol

TEACH Services, Inc.
Brushton, New York

**PRINTED IN
THE UNITED STATES OF AMERICA**

World rights reserved. This book or any portion thereof may not be copied or reproduced in any form or manner whatever, except as provided by law, without the written permission of the publisher, except by a reviewer who may quote brief passages in a review. The author assumes full responsibility for the accuracy of all facts and quotations as cited in this book.

2010 11 12 13 14 · 5 4 3 2 1

Copyright © 2010 Pedro M. Prestol and TEACH Services, Inc.
ISBN-13: 978-1-57258-618-5
ISBN-10: 1-57258-618-4
Library of Congress Control Number: 2009944147

Unless otherwise noted, all Scripture quotations in this book are from the *English Standard Version*.

Published by

TEACH Services, Inc.
www.TEACHServices.com

CONTENTS

WHY DO MOST CHRISTIANS WORSHIP ON SUNDAY?

Many Christian groups say that Sunday is the Christian Sabbath. They claim that God commanded us to observe the Sabbath, not on the seventh day, but on one day out of the seven. Other Christians say that the early church began meeting on Sunday in honor of the resurrection of Jesus, which took place on the first day of the week. That is why we no longer observe the Jewish Sabbath (Saturday) but worship instead on Sunday, a distinctively Christian holy day. Others say that we no longer have to keep the Ten Commandments, and therefore, Sabbath observance is not needed.

There are many opinions, but have you examined the Holy Scriptures and confirmed it as a fact? Does it matter on which day you worship? Should we as Christians keep the Sabbath or Sunday holy? Was the Sabbath changed from the seventh to the first day of the week by Jesus or the apostles? In this book, I will cover all aspects of the arguments that I have heard on this subject. The evidence is present in the Scriptures! May the Holy Spirit guide you and lead you to the light of truth, which only the Word of God can provide.

MAN FALLS INTO SIN

The book of Genesis describes how God created the heavens and the earth. On the sixth day of creation, God created man: "Then God said, 'Let us make man in our image, after our likeness. And let them have dominion over the fish of the sea and over the birds of the heavens and over the livestock and over all the earth and over every creeping thing that creeps on the earth.' So God created man in his own image, in the image of God he created him; male and female he created them" (Genesis 1:26-27).

God commanded Adam and Eve not to eat from the tree of the knowledge of good and evil: "The LORD God took the man and put him in the garden of Eden to work it and keep it. And the LORD God commanded the man, saying, 'You may surely eat of every tree of the garden, but of the tree of the knowledge of good and evil you shall not eat, for in the day that you eat of it you shall surely die'" (Genesis 2:15-17).

Satan, hearing this direct command from God to Adam and Eve, used the serpent to deceive Eve into eating the fruit, thereby disobeying God: "He said to the woman, 'Did God actually say, "You shall not eat of any tree in the garden"?' And the woman said to the serpent, 'We may eat of the fruit of the trees in the garden, but God said, "You shall not eat of the fruit of the tree that is in the midst of the garden, neither shall you touch it, lest you die."' But the serpent said to the woman, 'You will not surely die'" (Genesis 3:1-4).

Friend, this is the most unfortunate event in the history of this world. Because of this event, we must face death. The Bible says that whosoever commits sin belongs to Satan: "He that committeth sin is of the devil; for the devil sinneth from the beginning" (1 John 3:8, KJV). Man sinned; therefore, man and the whole planet belonged to the devil. Fortunately, God had a plan to come and pay the price of sin by dying on the cross and saving mankind from their sins.

The Plan of Salvation

When Adam and Eve sinned, they were cast out of Eden; they had to die for their transgression, for the Bible says, "For the wages of sin is death" (Romans 6:23, NKJV). But what is sin? The Bible says, "Whosoever committeth sin transgresseth also the law: for sin is the transgression of the law" (1 John 3:4, KJV). Man sins when he disobeys God; Adam and Eve disobeyed God by eating the prohibited fruit. The consequence of their sin was death.

Yet, that was not the end for man, because God had a plan. God gave His only son, Jesus, for humanity. The Bible says, "For God so loved the world, that he gave his only Son, that whoever believes in him should not perish but have eternal life" (John 3:16). If you believe in Jesus' sacrifice on the cross and accept His gift, your sins will be forgiven.

After Adam and Eve fell into sin, God clothed them with skins because they were able to see their nakedness: "Unto Adam also and to his wife did the LORD God make coats of skins, and clothed them" (Genesis 3:21, KJV). This was the first record of death in Scripture. After all, the wages of sin is death. God became the first one to kill the first sacrifice—a poor innocent lamb—to cover the nakedness of men. What a lesson!

Adam and Eve must have felt horrible. Because of their disobedience, creation was condemned. By killing the lamb, God promised man that one day the real Lamb of God, whom we now know as Jesus Christ, our Lord and Savior, would come to earth and pay for our sins once and for all. With His death, He gave us life. The lamb symbolized the Messiah, who was offered because of our transgressions. If Adam and Eve had not disobeyed God, there would have been no need for a sacrifice or shedding of blood, and Adam and Eve would have stayed in perfect communion with God, doing His will and keeping His commandments. Yet, since they sinned, they needed a way to receive forgiveness, and God showed them how by sacrificing a lamb.

Men have always struggled with doing what they want versus obeying the Lord. Take for example Cain and Abel. God had already shown them that they had to sacrifice a lamb as an offering to Him. The Bible says, "And Abel, he also brought of the firstlings of his flock and of the fat thereof. And the LORD had respect unto Abel and to his offering" (Genesis 4:4, KJV). God accepted what Abel brought because that is what God had asked the first family to do, but Cain brought what he wanted. God did not accept Cain's offering: "But unto Cain and to his offering he had not respect" (verse 5).

The same thing happens today. Since the creation of the world, God has asked us to keep His Sabbath holy, which is the seventh day of the week, but many people want to observe another day of the week instead. Do you not think that God will have the same reaction to your offering as He did to Cain's? He did not ask for fruits, neither did He ask for any other day of the week but the seventh!

The Creation

Some Christians believe that the Sabbath was for the Jewish nation only. I have one question: Were Adam and Eve Jewish? Of course not. There was no nation at that time, just mankind. This means the Sabbath was for mankind. Jesus Himself said, "The sabbath was made for man, and not man for the sabbath" (Mark 2:27, KJV).

The Sabbath serves multiple purposes: 1) to confirm the true story of Creation; 2) it clearly leads to the theory of the existence of God; 3) to give us rest from our weekly labor as performed on the other days; and 4) to worship Jehovah, the Creator of the heavens and earth. The Sabbath, apart from the other days, is the only one that God named. This can be confirmed by the Hebrew names for the days of the week. Keep in mind that the Hebrews were the twelve children of Israel, and their customs were not of pagan origin like other nations.

The table below presents the days of the week, their names and Hebrew meanings.

יום רִאשׁוֹן	יוֹם שֵׁנִי	יוֹם שְׁלִישִׁי	יוֹם רְבִיעִי	יוֹם חֲמִישׁי	יוֹם שִׁשִּׁי	יוֹם שַׁבָּת
yom rishon	yom sheyni	yom shlishi	yom revi'i	yom khamishi	yom shishi	yom Shabbat
(First day)	(Second day)	(Third day)	(Fourth day)	(Fifth day)	(Sixth day)	(Sabbath-day)

Did you know that God created everything in six days, and on the seventh day, He rested? He did not name any of the days, but on the seventh day, the Bible says that God rested. This is exactly why the seventh day is called *Yom Shabbat* in Hebrew, which means "day of rest." Let us analyze the Bible verse more thoroughly. The Bible says, "Thus the heavens and the earth were finished, and all the host of them. And on the seventh day God ended his work which he had made; and he rested on the seventh day from all his work which he had made. And God blessed the seventh day, and sanctified it: because that in it he had rested from all his work which God created and made" (Genesis 2:1-3, KJV).

Did you notice the two things God did to the seventh day that He did not do to the other days or to anything else He created? He blessed the seventh day and sanctified it! According to the *Merriam-Webster Dictionary*, "blessed" means "held in reverence, honored in worship. —Venerated: to honor (as an icon or a relic) with a ritual act of devotion."

What about "sanctified," what does that mean? According to the Merriam-Webster Dictionary, it means "to set apart to a sacred purpose." This is something done by God, not by man. We have to keep in mind that sin had not yet entered the world, so there was no ritual or ceremonial association of the weekly Sabbath to the Sabbaths of the Ceremonial Laws, which were given to Moses many years later on Mount Sinai. Adam and Eve kept the first Sabbath with God. I also believe that they kept the other nine Commandments. How do I know this? From the simple fact that Adam and Eve did not steal, kill, or worship any false God, I believe we can safely say that the Ten Commandments were given to Adam and Eve in the Garden of Eden. Another fact to consider is that the fourth Commandment starts with the word "remember." People cannot be told to remember something unless it has been mentioned before.

Unfortunately, some individuals try to disprove that there is a God who created the heavens and the earth, thus justifying their own ideas and their disobedient behavior. For example, the late Pope John Paul II supported the theory of evolution. John Paul II said, "New knowledge leads us to recognize in the theory of evolution more than a hypothesis" (New Advent, http://www.newadvent.org/library/docs_jp02tc.htm, [accessed October 16, 2009]). Even the current pope, Pope Benedict XVI, has made declarations in support of the evolution theory as a fact. He said, "This contrast is an absurdity, because there are many scientific tests in favor of evolution, which appears as a reality that we must see and enriches our understanding of life and being" (Bill Sanderson, *New York Post*, July 26, 2007).

Do you realize what they are trying to imply? They are trying to imply that the book of Genesis is a lie! If what the book of Genesis records is not true, the origin of the weekly Sabbath cannot be proven with the Bible, making it easier for individuals to make the change from the seventh day Sabbath to Sunday. Most importantly, the true God who created it cannot be revealed! People who do not follow the Bible will do anything possible to convince the world that their forgery is truth! They seek to blind the ignorant and mislead the unwary.

The Biblical Sabbath

The true Sabbath is first found in the book of Genesis, in which Moses, inspired by the Holy Spirit, narrates the Creation story—the beginning of this planet. In six days, God created the heavens and the earth, and on the seventh day, He rested. "Thus the heavens and the earth were finished, and all the host of them. And on the seventh day God ended his work which he had made; and he rested on the seventh day from all his work which he had made. And God blessed the seventh day, and sanctified it: because that in it he had rested from all his work which God created and made" (Genesis 2:1-3, KJV).

As I previously mentioned, the Sabbath is not just for the Jews, since Adam and Eve were not Jewish and no nation had been established yet. Another teaching that veers away from biblical doctrine is that the Sabbath was a ceremonial ritual. When God first gave the Sabbath to Adam and Eve, sin did not yet exist. So how could the weekly Sabbath be a ceremonial ritual when as yet there was no sin? Many Christians do not understand the difference between the moral law (Ten Commandments) and the Ceremonial Law (the book of the law). They just think it is one whole law. Nothing could be further from the truth. Let me explain their differences.

THE CEREMONIAL AND MORAL LAWS: TWO DIFFERENT LAWS

The Ceremonial Law was given by God to Moses as a promise that the Messiah would come and die for man's sin. Paul said: "For since the law has but a shadow of the good things to come instead of the true form of these realities, it can never, by the same sacrifices that are continually offered every year, make perfect those who draw near" (Hebrews 10:1).

Paul, in other words, is saying that the Book of the Law is nothing but a representation of Jesus. God told Moses: "Speak to the people of Israel, saying, If anyone sins unintentionally in any of the LORD's commandments about things not to be done, and does any one of them, if it is the anointed priest who sins, thus bringing guilt on the people, then he shall offer for the sin that he has committed a bull from the herd without blemish to the LORD for a sin offering" (Leviticus 4:2-3).

Paul gives more evidence of this by saying: "You have neither desired nor taken pleasure in sacrifices and offerings and burnt offerings and sin offerings (these are offered according to the law)" (Hebrews 10:8). Paul is referring to the Mosaic Law, which also included the Ceremonial Laws. Nowhere in the Ten Commandments will you find any command to burn any offerings. Evidently, Paul is talking about the Book of the Law (Ceremonial Law). This was a prophetic book that pointed to the Messiah's sacrifice.

Jesus said: "These are my words that I spoke to you while I was still with you, that everything written about me in the Law of Moses and the Prophets and the Psalms must be fulfilled" (Luke 24:44). Others who knew the Book of the Law understood it this way as well: "Philip found Nathanael and said to him, 'We have found him of whom Moses in the Law and also the prophets wrote, Jesus of Nazareth, the son of Joseph" (John 1:45).

7

As you can see, the Bible shows that the Book of the Law prophesied the coming of the Messiah, but I ask the question again: What is sin? Let the Bible give us the answer. It says, "Whosoever committeth sin transgresseth also the law: for sin is the transgression of the law" (1 John 3:4, KJV). Which law do you think the apostle John is referring to? The Ten Commandments! You might wonder why. Well, the Bible says, "For whoever keeps the whole law but fails in one point has become accountable for all of it. For he who said, 'Do not commit adultery,' also said, 'Do not murder.' If you do not commit adultery but do murder, you have become a transgressor of the law" (James 2:10-11). James is clearly quoting the Ten Commandments here.

Yes, dear reader, breaking the law of God, which is the Ten Commandments, is sin. Keep in mind that honoring the Sabbath is the fourth commandment, and Sunday is not the Sabbath; it is the first day of the week. If you observe Sunday as the Sabbath, you are not following the commandment of God, and therefore, you are disobeying God.

The Book of the Law was written by Moses: "Just as Moses the servant of the LORD had commanded the people of Israel, as it is written in the Book of the Law of Moses" (Joshua 8:31, NKJV); "When Moses had finished writing the words of this law in a book to the very end" (Deuteronomy 31:24).

As you can see, the Ceremonial Law, also known as the Mosaic Law, was written by Moses in a book. Yet, the Ten Commandments were written in stone by God. "The LORD said to Moses, 'Come up to me on the mountain and wait there, that I may give you the tablets of stone, with the law and the commandment, which I have written for their instruction'" (Exodus 24:12).

Do you see the difference? They are two different laws. The weekly Sabbath is found in the tablets of stone, written by God. Why do you think God wrote His law in stone? God wrote His law in stone as a symbol that His

8

law cannot be erased or changed, and since He wrote it, it cannot be destroyed! Since the law of God cannot be abolished, Jesus gave His life for our transgressions. Jesus came to fulfill the Book of the Law.

Jesus said, "Do not think that I have come to abolish the Law or the Prophets; I have not come to abolish them but to fulfill them" (Matthew 5:17). Paul said, "For I delivered to you as of first importance what I also received: that Christ died for our sins in accordance with the Scriptures" (1 Corinthians 15:3). Which scripture is Paul talking about? It is the Book of the Law, written by Moses, as I have already explained. It is clear in the Scriptures that the Ceremonial Law is not the same as the Moral Law. The fourth commandment from the law of God is the Sabbath, which is part of that Moral Law.

THE EARTHLY AND HEAVENLY SANCTUARIES

Before Jesus' sacrifice for our sins on the cross of Calvary, how could mankind obtain forgiveness for their sins? In a previous section, I showed how God taught Adam and Eve that a lamb had to be offered. During Moses' time, God needed to have these rules written down; therefore, He used Moses. With the Ceremonial Laws, man knew exactly what to do when he sinned, but a sanctuary was needed for these ritual purposes. God gave Moses instructions on how to build this sanctuary. It was divided into two sections called the holy place and the Most Holy Place. "And you shall hang the veil from the clasps, and bring the ark of the testimony in there within the veil. And the veil shall separate for you the Holy Place from the Most Holy" (Exodus 26:33).

In this verse, we can see that God is giving Moses instructions on how to build the Sanctuary. The holy place was used for the daily sacrifices. In its interior, it contained the lampstand with seven lamps and the table for the bread of proposition. "For a tent was prepared, the first section, in which were the lampstand and the table and the bread of the Presence. It is called the Holy Place" (Hebrews 9:2). The second section was called the Most Holy Place. "Behind the second curtain was a second section called the Most Holy Place, having the golden altar of incense and the Ark of the Covenant covered on all sides with gold, in which was a golden urn holding the manna, and Aaron's staff that budded, and the tablets of the covenant" (verses 3–4).

The Most Holy Place was entered only once a year, where an offering was made on behalf of the nation. This was called the Day of Atonement, or Yom Kippur. The Ten Commandments were placed inside the ark of the covenant in the Most Holy Place; the Book of the Law was placed outside the ark. The Bible says, "Moses commanded the Levites who carried the ark of the covenant of the LORD, 'Take this Book of the Law and put it by the side of the ark of the covenant of the LORD your God, that it may be there for a witness against you'" (Deuteronomy 31:25–26).

The placing of the two tablets of stone inside the ark and the Book of the Law outside is another piece of evidence regarding their nature and purposes. The earthly sanctuary was a mere copy of the heavenly sanctuary, as the Bible says, "And let them make me a sanctuary, that I may dwell in their midst. Exactly as I show you concerning the pattern of the tabernacle, and of all its furniture, so you shall make it" (Exodus 25:8–9). God showed Moses the heavenly sanctuary and asked him to make a copy here on earth. God has His sanctuary in heaven; just like the earthly sanctuary, it is divided in two sections, and God's holy ark of the covenant is inside the Most Holy Place with God's Ten Commandments. The apostle Paul tells us: "For Christ has entered, not into holy places made with hands, which are copies of the true things, but into heaven itself, now to appear in the presence of God on our behalf" (Hebrews 9:24). "Then God's temple in heaven was opened, and the ark of his covenant was seen within his temple" (Revelation 11:19).

The ark of the covenant is where the Ten Commandments lie. Yes, without a doubt, the Ten Commandments still stand in heaven and, therefore, also on earth. The Sabbath is in effect now just as it was at the end of Creation and at Mount Sinai, and it will continue in heaven after the second coming of Christ. The observance of the Sabbath will be for eternity, for the Bible says, "'For as the new heavens and the new earth that I make shall remain before me, says the LORD, so shall your offspring and your name remain. From new moon to new moon, and from Sabbath to Sabbath, all flesh shall come to worship before me, declares the LORD" (Isaiah 66:22–23).

Some people might say, "New moon? Feast of the new moons?" No, this is not talking about a feast. New moon means new month, which is a way of keeping track of time. The original Hebrew word used here was *kho'-desh*, which means "the new moon; by implication a month: —month (-ly), new moon" (Strong's Hebrew and Greek dictionary, H2318).

The Gospel of Jesus

The Book of the Law, which we already identified as having been written by Moses, was a prophetic book that prophesied about the future Messiah, who would come and die for our sins. This Messiah was Jesus Christ. We no longer have to follow the ceremonial rituals from the Mosaic Law, since Jesus already fulfilled their purpose. After the death of Jesus, we have a new message to proclaim, as Paul said, "Be imitators of me, as I am of Christ" (1 Corinthians 11:1). Paul tells us to imitate him just like he imitates Christ. Since he asks this of us, we are going to look in the Scriptures for the things that Jesus did.

I'd like to go straight to the point. Did Jesus ever keep Sunday holy? Did Jesus give any sort of hint of a change in Sabbath observation from the seventh day to the first day of the week? Christians are called Christians because we ought to be imitators of Christ; therefore, we need to find out from the Scriptures if Jesus kept the Sabbath or Sunday. It does not matter what Ignatius of Antioch, Justin Martyr, your pastor, or anyone else has said or says. What matters is what Jesus says—do you agree with me? If we do not imitate Christ, then we are not Christians. The Bible says, "Whoever says he abides in him ought to walk in the same way in which he walked" (1 John 2:6).

Let us start with which day of the week Jesus taught in the synagogue. The Bible says, "And on the Sabbath he began to teach in the synagogue" (Mark 6:2). Jesus went to the synagogue on the Sabbath to teach. Was this something He did before or after He started His ministry, or was it something He always did? The Bible says, "And as was his custom, he went to the synagogue on the Sabbath day, and he stood up to read" (Luke 4:16). It was

Jesus' custom to go to the synagogue on the Sabbath, not on Sunday.

Jesus always kept the Sabbath holy. He is our ultimate example—God made man! Do you want to be an imitator of Jesus? If yes, then you need to keep the Sabbath holy, not Sunday.

Most Christian churches teach that the day of worship was changed from Sabbath to Sunday because Jesus rose from the dead on the first day of the week. In remembrance of that event, the church changed the solemnity of the Sabbath to Sunday. This is not what the Bible teaches. I will show evidence in later sections to back up this claim.

If Jesus had wanted to commemorate His resurrection by keeping Sunday holy, He would have told His apostles to do so. Yet, Jesus gave His apostles another act to do in remembrance of His death. The Bible says, "And he took bread, and when he had given thanks, he broke it and gave it to them, saying, 'This is my body, which is given for you. Do this in remembrance of me'" (Luke 22:19).

If Jesus took the time to show His disciples at the Last Supper what they needed to do in remembrance of His death, why didn't He show them that they needed to keep Sunday in remembrance of His resurrection? Simply, because Jesus never wanted it changed, and most importantly, the law of God cannot be changed. That is why Jesus died for us—because the law of God cannot be changed. If it could have been, He could have changed it, and death would have never entered the earth. You need to understand that the wages of sin is death, and sin is the transgression of the law of God. Furthermore, Jesus never said He was the Lord of Sunday but that He was Lord of the Sabbath: "For the Son of Man is lord of the Sabbath" (Matthew 12:8).

I know that there are people who believe and preach that the apostle John said in the book of Revelation, "I was in the Spirit on the Lord's day," referring to Sunday as the Lord's day. However, John was present and very aware when Jesus made the statement that He was Lord of the Sabbath. Do you think that John would be so irresponsible as to refer to Sunday as the Lord's day? Sunday was Dies Solis, "day of the sun," as the Romans called it. John knew that the first day of the week was the *dominus solis deis* (day of the lord sun) for the pagans. In this passage, John was talking about the true Lord, Jesus Christ, and the Sabbath, the seventh day of the week!

What about after Jesus' resurrection? Did Jesus give any hint of a future change? No, never; on the contrary, Jesus told His followers to keep the Sabbath even after His death. The Bible says, "Pray that your flight may not be in winter or on a Sabbath" (Matthew 24:20). Jesus was prophesying about the destruction of Jerusalem, which took place in the year AD 70, about thirty-nine years after His death. With this warning, Jesus was indicating that His followers needed to continue keeping the Sabbath holy even after He departed from this planet.

THE APOSTLES AND THE SABBATH DAY

Many people claim that it was the apostles who changed the Sabbath to Sunday. These individuals do not accept the fact that Sunday, as a holy day, is a pagan institution and the Roman Catholic Church made it a Christian holy day. Did the apostles really believe that after Jesus' death, Sunday became the new Christian Sabbath? We have already established that Jesus wanted His disciples to continue keeping the Sabbath holy even after His death. Would the apostles go against His will? I do not think so.

However, it is not what I think that matters. What matters is what the Scriptures tell us. We must, therefore, search the Scriptures to see for ourselves if the apostles kept Sunday or the Sabbath after Christ's death. If the apostles believed that Sunday was the new Sabbath after Christ's death, there should be evidence of this fact in their writings. Most churches today teach that the apostles kept Sunday instead of the Sabbath, but let us look in the Scriptures to see if that is true.

There are only eight verses that mention the first day of the week, and five of them are referring to the same event—Christ's resurrection. The apostles wrote their epistles years after Christ's death; therefore, if they believed that Sunday was the new Christian Sabbath, they would have referred to it as such in their epistles. Let us see if that is the case by starting with Matthew.

The Gospel According to Matthew

The first verse that mentions the first day of the week is found in the book of Matthew. It says, "Now after the Sabbath, toward the dawn of the first day of the week, Mary Magdalene and the other Mary went to see the tomb" (Matthew 28:1). Notice that the apostle calls the first day of the week by its proper name, the first day of the week, and the seventh day he calls the Sabbath. If he had believed that the seventh day Sabbath was not for Christianity but instead that the first day of the week was the Lord's day, then why did he not refer to it as such? Why did he not call the seventh day the seventh day? Because Matthew knew that the seventh day of the week was the Sabbath, and the first day was merely a day.

The *Encarta* encyclopedia says, "They [scholars] believed that he wrote the Gospel in Palestine, just prior to the destruction of Jerusalem in AD 70. Although this opinion is still held by some, most scholars consider the Gospel According to Mark the earliest Gospel" ("Gospel According to Matthew," in Microsoft® Encarta® Online Encyclopedia 2008).

The epistle of Matthew is the first book of the New Testament. As we confirmed with Encarta, it was written around the year AD 70. Jesus died in the year AD 31, so the epistle according to Matthew was written thirty-nine years after Christ's death. I believe that in thirty-nine years of study, Matthew would have discovered and written about any changes in the day of worship. Matthew evidently believed that the seventh day of the week was the Sabbath.

The Gospel According to Mark

The second verse to mention the first day of the week is found in the book of Mark. Mark is discussing the same event that Matthew discussed, but in his own words: "And very early on the first day of the week, when the sun had risen, they went to the tomb (Mark 16:2).

The third verse is also recorded in the book of Mark. It says, "Now when he rose early on the first day of the week, he appeared first to Mary Magdalene, from whom he had cast out seven demons" (Mark 16:9). Mark, just like Matthew, clearly calls the first day of the week simply the first day of the week.

The Encarta encyclopedia says, referring to its date of composition: "In chapter 13, Mark refers to the destruction of Jerusalem either as an event that may shortly happen or as one that has recently happened. Consequently, although scholars do not know whether to date the Gospel shortly before or shortly after AD 70, it is virtually certain that it is not far removed from that date" ("Microsoft® Encarta® Online Encyclopedia 2008).

Jesus died in the year AD 31, and the book of Mark was written around AD 70, which was thirty-nine years later. If Mark held any sort of belief that the seventh day Sabbath was no longer the Lord's day and had been replaced by the first day of the week, I think thirty-nine years would have been enough time for him to have expressed or to have had a vision about the change. Mark, like Matthew, kept the Sabbath, and neither one called the first day of the week, Sunday, the Lord's day. Mark believed in and kept the Sabbath holy for the rest of his life, just as Jesus did.

The Gospel According to Luke

The fourth verse that mentions the first day of the week is found in the book of Luke. Is it possible that Matthew and Mark never found out about the change? Luke relates: "But on the first day of the week, at early dawn, they went to the tomb, taking the spices they had prepared" (Luke 24:1). Luke, just like the other apostles, called the first day of the week the first day of the week.

The Encarta encyclopedia provides the following information regarding the composition date of the gospel of Luke: "It is now generally agreed that the Gospel of Luke dates from the decade AD 70 to 80. Earlier or later dates have also been proposed: if, as some have suggested, Acts was written while Paul was imprisoned in Rome, Luke's Gospel could have been written about 63 to 65; if the absence before then of any reference to the Gospel in the writings of the earliest Fathers of the Church is taken as proof of a later date, it is possible that Luke's Gospel was composed at the end of the 1st century. It is unknown whether the Gospel was written in Rome, Asia Minor, or

Greece" ("Gospel According to Luke," in Microsoft® Encarta® Online Encyclopedia 2008).

Like the other apostles, many years had passed by the time Luke wrote his epistle, and if there was any sort of change from the Sabbath to Sunday, Luke would have known about it. Obviously, Luke did not know of any such change, and therefore, he did not teach it. It is interesting to note that Luke was Greek ("Saint Luke," in *The Catholic Encyclopedia*). Luke, a Gentile, referred to the seventh day of the week as the Sabbath many years after Christ's death. He remained faithful to the teachings of Jesus.

The Gospel According to John

The fifth verse that mentions the first day of the week is found in the gospel according to John. John says, "Now on the first day of the week Mary Magdalene came to the tomb early, while it was still dark, and saw that the stone had been taken away from the tomb" (John 20:1).

Encarta has the following to say about the year of its composition: "Most moderate scholars now date John from sometime in the last decade of the 1st century or early in the 2nd century" ("Gospel According to John," in Microsoft® Encarta® Online Encyclopedia 2008).

Again and again, all of the apostles called the first day of the week, just as they were supposed to, the first day of the week. Do you remember the verse in the book of Revelation in which John says he was on the "Lord's day"? Why then does he not call it the Lord's day when he was talking about Christ's resurrection? Because John never called the first day of the week the Lord's day! He called the seventh day of the week, which is the true Lord's day, the Lord's day. These verses were the first five verses to mention the first day of the week, and they all recorded the same event—the resurrection of Jesus on the first day of the week.

There are three verses left that mention the first day of the week, and most Sunday-keepers use them as evidence that the apostles gathered on the first day of the week to worship. But, as we have so far read, we have not found a doctrinal basis in the Scriptures for Sunday-keeping. If the apostles had such a belief, they would have indicated it in their writings, which they so far have not.

The sixth verse that mentions the first day of the week is also found in the book of John. It says, "On the evening of that day, the first day of the week, the doors being locked where the disciples were for fear of the Jews, Jesus came and stood among them and said to them, 'Peace be with you'" (John 20:19). This verse is well used among Sunday advocates. They claim that this verse indicates that the apostles were worshipping on the first day of the week. But notice that it starts by saying "on the evening of that day." Which day? The first day of the week, of course. Remember that in the beginning God established that a day goes from sundown to sundown; this can also be proved by the way in which the Jews continue to count a full day. The Bible says, "So the evening and the morning were the first day" (Genesis 1:5, NKJV).

Therefore, although the apostles were gathered together on the first day, technically the second day had already began. They were also hiding away from the Jews. It was Sunday night; to the Jews, it was already the next day. Jesus appeared and said, "Peace be with you." Many people believe that since Jesus appeared to the apostles for the first time in the event recorded by this verse, it was a sign that Jesus had approved Sunday as the new day of worship. However, according to the timeframe discussed above as outlined in Genesis, Jesus appeared to them on Sunday night, which was the start of Monday, the second day of the week. Another thing we need to notice in this verse is that it only says "they were gathered"; since it does not specify what type of gathering it was, one cannot assert that it was a worship gathering. The poor apostles were so depressed over Jesus' death that they did not know what to do. Thus, Jesus came to their rescue in their darkest hour.

Acts of the Apostles

The next verse that mentions the first day of the week is found in the book of Acts. This is the one verse that most Christians use as an evidence to try to prove that the apostles started the tradition of Sunday worship.

"Scholars agree that the Acts of the Apostles was written by the same person who wrote the Gospel of Luke. Some scholars have reasoned therefore that the book was written before Paul's death (circa 61) and before the collection of his letters early in the 2nd century. Because the Acts is designed to serve as a second volume, however, the book must be at least slightly later than the Gospel of Luke, and the Gospel is almost certainly later than that of Mark. The result is to put Luke's two volumes sometime in the last two decades of the 1st century" ("Acts of the Apostles," in Microsoft® Encarta® Online Encyclopedia 2008).

This next text is often used by individuals who are trying to prove that the apostles, as well as Paul, were keeping the first day of the week as the Christian Sabbath. But let us look closely at what the Bible says: "And upon the first day of the week, when the disciples came together to break bread, Paul preached unto them, ready to depart on the morrow; and continued his speech until midnight." (Acts 20:7). KJV

The first thing that must be pointed out is that this author, as well as the others that we have discussed so far, called it "the first day of the week." He did not call it the Lord's day or the Sabbath; no, he called it by its right name, the first day of the week. Second, they were together breaking bread. This did not mean that some special event was taking place; it simply meant that they had gathered together to eat. Third, most scholars do not come to an agreement on which method Luke used to measure the day. Was it the Jewish method or the Roman method? If it was the Jewish one, then the meeting started Saturday night, and if it was the Roman one, then it started Sunday night. Finally, the reason why this event was recorded was not because they broke bread but because Paul resurrected the young man who fell from the window.

Breaking bread is something we all do every day, but resurrecting someone from the dead is something only God can do. This is an important story documenting a wonderful miracle! Paul was evangelizing in Troas, and the person narrating the story began the story from when they were breaking bread. The author mentions the disciples. People frequently think that these disciples were the twelve apostles of Christ, but in actuality, they were not. Notice that it says, "Paul preached unto them." Did the apostles need Paul to preach to them? The original Greek word use for disciples here is *mathētēs*, meaning "a learner, this is, pupil: —disciple (Strong's Hebrew and Greek dictionary, G3129).

These "disciples" were the people of Troas who were there to learn from Paul. The apostles were not worshipping on Sunday, and Paul was not teaching the people of Troas to worship on Sunday. The focus of the story is on the fact that Paul resurrected a young man from the dead. It is not mentioned anywhere in the verse that one should break bread every Sunday. Furthermore, there is no evidence in this verse for Sunday keeping, but there is plenty of evidence for keeping the Sabbath holy.

Did the apostle Paul keep the Sabbath or Sunday holy?

The last verse to mention the first day of the week is found in the book of Corinthians, which was authored by Paul. It says, "On the first day of every week, each of you is to put something aside and store it up, as he may prosper, so that there will be no collecting when I come" (1 Corinthians 16:2). Some Christians teach that because Paul told them to "put something aside" Paul was collecting some kind of offering. Since this collection was on the first day of the week, these individuals believe that this verse indicates that they were participating in some type of worship service, at which time an offering was collected. Is there any truth in such teachings?

Let's look at the next verse carefully. Paul continues, "When I arrive, I will send those whom you accredit by letter to carry your gift to Jerusalem" (verse 3). If they were in a worship service why would they send someone to retrieve the offering? They, therefore, cannot be in a worship meeting.

These verses are not talking about a worship service, instead they are discussing special donations that were collected for the brethren in Jerusalem who were going through hard times. Paul confirms this by giving praise to two churches for their contributions: "I am going to Jerusalem bringing aid to the saints. For Macedonia and Achaia have been pleased to make a some contribution for the poor among the saints at Jerusalem" (Romans 15:25-26).

As you can see from all the verses in the New Testament that mention the first day of the week, there is no evidence in the Bible to support the idea that the apostles worshiped on the first day of the week. It is clear that the early church after the death of Christ kept the true Sabbath holy. In fact, additional passages support the fact that Paul kept the true Sabbath. The Bible says, "And when the Jews were gone out of the synagogue, the Gentiles besought that these words might be preached to them the next sabbath." (Acts 13:42, KJV).

As you can see from this verse, the author refers to the seventh day of the week as the Sabbath. If Paul had believed that the Sabbath was not binding anymore, why would he call it the Sabbath? Indeed, on the next Sabbath they met again! The Bible says, "And the next sabbath day came almost the whole city together to hear the word of God" (verse 44, KJV).

If the Sabbath was for the Jews alone, why were the Gentiles asking to meet again on the next Sabbath? If the Sabbath was not for the Gentiles, then why did Paul agree to meet with them on the next Sabbath?

The assertion made by some that the Sabbath was for the children of Israel cannot be backed up by the Bible. The Sabbath is for mankind! This is made clear by the following four points: 1) the Sabbath is the day on which God rested from all His works of creation, 2) Adam and Eve were not Jewish, 3) Jesus kept the Sabbath, and 4) we will continue to keep the Sabbath in heaven. Furthermore, Paul says, "There is neither Jew nor Greek, there is neither bond nor free, there is neither male nor female: for ye are all one in Christ Jesus" (Galatians 3:28, KJV). We are all one in Jesus. Jesus created everything, including the Sabbath, and while on earth, He said, "The Sabbath was made for man, not man for the Sabbath" (Mark 2:27). The original Greek word used for "man" in this verse was *anthropos*— "ωψ ops (the countenance); man-faced, that is, a human being: —certain, man" (Strong's Hebrew and Greek dictionary, G435 and G3700).

God gave mankind the Sabbath as a day of rest, a day dedicated to worshipping Him. Of course, we can worship God on any day, but the Sabbath is a special day that God ordained to be dedicated to Him. It is the only day that God made holy and blessed! Furthermore, evidence that Paul kept the Sabbath is found in the book of Acts. The Bible says, "And on the sabbath we went out of the city by a river side, where prayer was wont to be made; and we sat down, and spake unto the women which resorted thither" (Acts 16:13, KJV). This verse indicates that Paul and his companions were keeping the true Sabbath and were looking for a place to worship God on His holy day. They went to a place that they knew was accustomed to worship on the Sabbath.

I know this because of the word "wont," which in the original Greek is *nomizo*—"properly to do by law (usage), that is, to accustom (passively be usual); by extension to deem or regard: —suppose, think, be wont" (Strong's Hebrew and Greek dictionary, G3551).

One final note concerning Paul and the Sabbath: While preaching to the Hebrews, Paul tells them to enter God's rest. This can be found in chapter 4 of the book of Hebrews. Paul is referring to two types of rest here. The first is Jesus Christ, our rest from sin, and the second is the seventh day Sabbath, when we rest from our weekly labor.

After reviewing Scripture, it is clear that the apostles kept and taught the Sabbath even after Jesus' death. There is no evidence that they switched to Sunday.

DID JESUS NAIL THE TEN COMMANDMENTS TO THE CROSS?

Some Christian groups believe that Jesus abolished the Ten Commandments at the cross. They teach that the apostle Paul testifies about this abolishment in his writings. Is this true? Would Paul go against what Jesus and the other apostles taught? If the Ten Commandments were abolished are we free to kill, commit adultery, and steal? No, of course not.

Many churches and individuals claim that only the fourth commandment was abolished, therefore, justifying the observance of Sunday as a day of worship. I propose that either all Ten Commandments were abolished or none were.

An American evangelist once preached that "the Sabbath was binding in Eden, and it has been in force ever since. The fourth commandment begins with the word 'remember,' showing that the Sabbath already existed when God wrote the law on the tables of stone at Sinai. How can men claim that this one commandment has been done away with when they will admit that the other nine are still binding?" (D. L. Moody, *Weighed and Wanting*, pp. 47–48).

Another author, James Cardinal Gibbons said, "But you may read the Bible from Genesis to Revelation, and you will not find a single line authorizing the sanctification of Sunday. The Scriptures enforce the religious observance of Saturday, a day which we never sanctify" (*The Faith of our Fathers*, 88th ed., p. 89).

Today, in most Christian churches it is taught that the law was abolished, meaning the Ten Commandments. They do not differentiate between the Book of the Law and the Ten Commandments, and many use Paul's writings to suggest that the law was abolished. Yet they do not know to which law Paul is referring—the Book of the Law or the Ten Commandments—and since they do not know the difference between the two, they simply refer to both the book and the tablets of stone together as one law.

There is a huge difference between the Book of the Law and the Ten Commandments, and they serve different purposes, as I discussed earlier. Paul's writings are very complex. Here is what Peter said about Paul's writings: "And count the patience of our Lord as salvation, just as our beloved brother Paul also wrote to you according to the wisdom given him, as he does in all his letters when he speaks in them of these matters. There are some things in them that are hard to understand, which the ignorant and unstable twist to their own destruction, as they do the other Scriptures" (2 Peter 3:15-16).

These false Christians twist what Paul wrote, making claims that Paul taught that the Ten Commandments are now abolished, which is not what Paul actually did. Let us read what Paul said about men following such doctrines: "Desiring to be teachers of the law, without understanding either what they are saying or the things about which they make confident assertions" (1 Timothy 1:7).

Did Paul teach that the law was abolished or not? I have already explained that Paul kept the Sabbath, but let us continue our search of the Scriptures. First, we must find out what Jesus said about the Ceremonial Law, the law given to Moses. "Do not think that I have come to abolish the Law or the Prophets; I have not come to abolish them but to fulfill them" (Matthew 5:17). Jesus said this because the Book of the Law was a prophetic book that predicted the future and contained references to the Messiah and His death. Jesus said, "For all the Prophets and the Law prophesied until John" (Matthew 11:13). Jesus was not talking about the apostle John, but about John the Baptist. John the apostle had not yet prophesied anything when Jesus made this declaration. Jesus was referring to the prophets that had prophesied about the Messiah and the Ceremonial Law, which also foretold about the Messiah, Jesus Christ.

The Bible says, "And he said unto them, These are the words which I spake unto you, while I was yet with you, that all things must be fulfilled, which were written in the law of Moses, and in the prophets, and in the psalms, concerning me" (Luke 24:44, KJV). With this declaration, Jesus is evidently presenting Himself as the Messiah that the book of the law prophesied about. Those who knew the Law of Moses recognized Jesus as the Messiah, as we can see in the next text: "Philip found Nathanael and said to him, 'We have found him of whom Moses in the Law and also the prophets wrote, Jesus of Nazareth, the son of Joseph'" (John 1:45). The purpose of the Law of Moses was to point to the true Messiah, the true sacrificial lamb for our sins.

Now, let us see what Paul has to say about the law. Paul does not clarify in this verse to which law he is referring because he is talking to those that know the law. He said: "Or do you not know, brothers—for I am speaking to those who know the law—that the law is binding on a person only as long as he lives?" (Romans 7:1). Paul never had to clarify, while preaching to the Jews, which law he was talking about, because they knew the difference between the two, unlike today's Christians who do not. Paul says, "And by Him everyone who believes is freed from everything from which you could not be freed by the law of Moses" (Acts 13:39). Paul is saying that by Jesus we can be free from sin, a feat that the Ceremonial Law could not achieve.

Some Christians say, "We are under grace, and we no longer need to keep the law." They include the Ten Commandments in this "law," using the following quote as a foundation: "I do not nullify the grace of God, for if righteousness were through the law, then Christ died for no purpose" (Galatians 2:21). Notice that Paul just says the "law" and does not identify which "law." Keep in mind that he is talking to those who knew the two laws.

Let us analyze the following quote from Paul: "For it is not the hearers of the law who are righteous before

God, but the doers of the law who will be justified" (Romans 2:13). Did Paul just contradict himself? Did he not say that if righteousness was through the law then Christ died for no purpose? And now he says that the doers of the law are the righteous ones before God. Of course he did not contradict himself. In the first passage, Paul is referring to the Ceremonial Law, which is found in the Book of the Law written by Moses; in the other passage, he is talking about the Ten Commandments, which were written by God.

Another passage used out of context is the following: "Now it is evident that no one is justified before God by the law, for 'The righteous shall live by faith'" (Galatians 3:11). Just as in the earlier passage, Paul is referring to the Ceremonial Law that was intended to take away sin, which was simply a representation of Jesus' sacrifice for our sins. Another reason for which I am sure that Paul is referring to the Ceremonial Law is because in verse 13 of the same chapter, he says, "Christ redeemed us from the curse of the law by becoming a curse for us—for it is written, 'Cursed is everyone who is hanged on a tree.'" Some Christians claim that Paul calls the Ten Commandments a curse due to the above passage. But do the Ten Commandments command a person to be hanged on a tree? Paul is quoting the Book of the Law. You can read the original passage in Deuteronomy 21:23.

If the Ten Commandments were abolished, as some suggest, then everyone is without sin, meaning that everyone is going to heaven. Paul said, "But where there is no law there is no transgression" (Romans 4:15). In other words, where there is no law there is no sin. The Bible testifies that all have sinned, meaning all mankind. The Bible says, "All have sinned and fall short of the glory of God" (Romans 3:23). Based on Scripture, it is clear that the law of God was not abolished. Unfortunately, Satan does his best to twist the truth, and he has tried to convince people throughout the ages that the Ten Commandments, including the fourth commandment, are no longer necessary. Satan knows that if you break one commandment, you are guilty of all.

The Bible says, "For whoever keeps the whole law but fails in one point has become accountable for all of it. For he who said, 'Do not commit adultery,' also said, 'Do not murder.' If you do not commit adultery but do murder, you have become a transgressor of the law" (James 2:10-11). You only have to break one of the Ten Commandments to be a sinner, and what easier way has Satan devised than to make man sin by switching the seventh day Sabbath to the first day of the week?

JUDGMENT DAY

I'm sure we have all heard of the judgment day. Preachers love to use this topic as a tool to frighten people, thinking it will bring them to Christ. However, those same preachers who preach one Sunday morning about the judgment day will preach the next Sunday from the same pulpit that there is "no law" and that "Christians do not need to keep the Ten Commandments—we have a higher calling."

Let's consider the judgment day topic. Logically speaking, in order to judge someone, there has to be a law in place to follow. This is further proof that Jesus did not abolish the law at the cross. Let's examine what the Bible says about the judgment day: "For God will bring every deed into judgment, with every secret thing, whether good or evil" (Ecclesiastes 12:14), and "The clamor will resound to the ends of the earth, for the LORD has an indictment against the nations; he is entering into judgment with all flesh, and the wicked he will put to the sword, declares the LORD" (Jeremiah 25:31).

These Bible texts indicate that God will judge everyone and put "the wicked to the sword," meaning a penalty which is death. Do we, mankind, have a better legal system than God? If you break a law on earth, you are taken to court to be judged, prosecuted, and sentenced, if found guilty. Likewise, God judges mankind according to the law. The Bible says, "So speak and so act as those who are to be judged under the law of liberty" (James 2:12).

The law of liberty to which James is referring is the Ten Commandments. As an example, let's say I committed murder and was taken to judgment. The judge says, "Pedro Miguel Prestol, you are found guilty of murder and the penalty for your transgression is the electric chair."

Fortunately, as Christians, we are represented by Jesus, and He defends us in the courts of heaven. In the heavenly court system, Jesus stands up and says, "Your Honor, Pedro is a new creature and has repented for his wrongdoing. Will you not, please, forgive him and spare his life?"

The Judge replies, "He committed a crime for which he must pay, and the law states that he needs to pay with his life."

Jesus turns and, with His gentle eyes, stares into mine. With His melodious voice, he says, "Your Honor, I know the law and because laws create order, and my Father is a God of order and my kingdom has order, I will pay his penalty. I will die in the electric chair for Pedro."

Friend, Jesus died on the cross for your sins. He paid the penalty of breaking the law of God. All you have to do is accept the gift of life that He has given you. Death entered our world because of one man's transgression: Adam. Fortunately, Jesus paid the ultimate penalty with His life so we can have eternal life through Him. Paul says, "For if by one man's trespass, death reigned through that one man, much more will those who receive the abundance of grace and the free gift of righteousness reign in life through the one man Jesus Christ" (Romans 5:17).

If the Ten Commandments had been abolished, as many Christian groups teach, why would God punish man? Where there is no law, there is no sin. And we all know that there is a lot of sin in this world. Jesus is going to condemn man for not keeping God's law. The Bible says, "Who is to condemn? Christ Jesus is the one who died—more than that, who was raised—who is at the right hand of God, who indeed is interceding for us" (Romans 8:34). The good news is that Jesus is currently interceding for us in the heavenly sanctuary! But we must do our part. We must confess our sins and ask the Father for forgiveness through Christ Jesus. We must repent for any laws we have broken.

We must listen to the Word of God and not turn away our ears. The earth will be destroyed because man has transgressed the law of God, including changing the forth commandment. Jesus said, "Many will say to me in that day, Lord, Lord, have we not prophesied in thy name? and in thy name have cast out devils? and in thy name done many wonderful works? And then will I profess unto them, I never knew you: depart from me, ye that work iniquity"[1] (Matthew 7:22-23, KJV).

The Bible says, "The earth also is defiled under the inhabitants thereof; because they have transgressed the laws,[2] changed the ordinance,[3] broken the everlasting covenant.[4] Therefore hath the curse devoured the earth, and they that dwell therein are desolate: therefore the

---

1   The original Greek word used for "iniquity" is *anomia* —an-om-ee'-ah — "[illegality, that is, violation of law or (generally) wickedness: —iniquity, X transgress (-ion of) the law, unrighteousness.]" (Strong's Hebrew and Greek dictionary, G459). In other words, Jesus will tell those that think they serve Him, but transgress the law of God, "I never knew you: depart from me, ye that transgress the Ten Commandments."

2   The original Hebrew word used here was: *torah torah*; "to-raw', to-raw; a precept or statute, especially the Decalogue or Pentateuch: —law" (Strong's Hebrew and Greek dictionary, H3384).

3   The original Hebrew word used here was: *choq*; "khoke; an enactment; hence an appointment (of time, space, quantity, labor or usage): —appointed, bound, commandment, convenient, custom, decree (-d), due, law, measure, X necessary, ordinance (-nary), portion, set time, statute, task" (Strong's Hebrew and Greek dictionary, H2710).

4   God showed Isaiah in vision why He was destroying the earth. Isaiah 24:5 says, "The earth also is defiled under the inhabitants thereof; because they have transgressed the laws [Decalogue], changed the ordinance [the fourth commandment], broken the everlasting covenant."

inhabitants of the earth are burned, and few men left" (Isaiah 24:5-6, KJV).

John said, "Whoever says, 'I know him,' but does not keep his commandments is a liar, and the truth is not in him" (1 John 2:4), and "By this we know that we love the children of God, when we love God and obey his commandments" (1 John 5:2).

Dear reader, the Ten Commandments have been in place since the beginning of the world, and it is the law of God that creates order in the universe. God will judge everyone by His law.

HOW DO I KEEP THE SABBATH HOLY?

Now that we have established that the seventh day of the week is the Sabbath of Jehovah, how do we, as God's servants, keep it holy? Let us again look to the Bible for an answer:

"If you turn back your foot from the Sabbath, from doing your pleasure on my holy day, and call the Sabbath a delight and the holy day of the LORD honorable; if you honor it, not going your own ways, or seeking your own pleasure, or talking idly; then you shall take delight in the LORD, and I will make you ride on the heights of the earth; I will feed you with the heritage of Jacob your father, for the mouth of the LORD has spoken" (Isaiah 58:13-14).

God tells us exactly how He wants us to keep the Sabbath holy, and He also tells us the blessings we shall receive if we do. What a gracious God! Many Christians today believe that Sabbath keepers teach that the Sabbath ought to be kept like the Pharisees did. However, just because the Pharisees distorted God's word does not mean God's word is void. Let us analyze the fourth commandment. God said:

"Remember the Sabbath day, to keep it holy. Six days you shall labor, and do all your work, but the seventh day is a Sabbath to the LORD your God. On it you shall not do any work, you, or your son, or your daughter, your male servant, or your female servant, or your livestock, or the sojourner who is within your gates. For in six days the LORD made heaven and earth, the sea, and all that is in them, and rested on the seventh day. Therefore the LORD blessed the Sabbath day and made it holy" (Exodus 20:8-11).

God gave mankind six days to do everything man needs to do so that he can rest and dedicate the seventh entirely to His service. As I have said before, we are called Christians because we are imitators of Christ. Then, how did Jesus Christ keep the Sabbath? Did He observe the

Sabbath like the Pharisees or differently? Jesus rejected the Pharisaical interpretation of the Sabbath and kept it differently.

Following is a brief outline of what Jesus did on the Sabbath day, giving us the correct concept on how to keep the Sabbath: Jesus went to the synagogue, healed the sick, and preached the word of God. From these three things, we can see that Jesus did not do His own will but that of His Father.

Looking at Genesis, we understand that the Sabbath starts at sunset on the sixth day and ends at sunset on the seventh day. The sixth day, known as the day of preparation in the Scriptures, is the day Sabbath keepers get ready for the Sabbath, including cooking and cleaning. The Sabbath is met with songs, prayers, and worship of our Lord, the creator of the Sabbath— we do not worship the Sabbath; we worship its Creator.

The Jews were taught false philosophies by the doctors of the law, and the Sabbath was overloaded with human traditions. Jesus once said, "This people honors me with their lips, but their heart is far from me; in vain do they worship me, teaching as doctrines the commandments of men" (Matthew 15:8-9). As Jesus stated in His own words, the Jewish leaders were teaching the commandments of men, and therefore, they accused Jesus of breaking the Sabbath. On one occasion Jesus healed a woman on the Sabbath, and one of the rulers of the synagogue became angry. The Bible relates the story: "But the ruler of the synagogue, indignant because Jesus had healed on the Sabbath, said to the people, 'There are six days in which work ought to be done. Come on those days and be healed, and not on the Sabbath day'" (Luke13:14).

Jesus said to them, "I ask you, is it lawful on the Sabbath to do good or to do harm, to save life or to destroy it?" (Luke 6:9). It is clear that Jesus observed the Sabbath by doing His Father's will. "The Sabbath was made for man, not man for the Sabbath" (Mark 2:27).

I urge you to read the Bible for yourself. Don't follow man and traditions, but follow God and His Word.

THE WORD SUNDAY

Did you know that the word "Sunday" is not found in the Bible? Not even once! We call the first day of the week Sunday; almost all Christian churches hold their worship services on this day, and it is called the Lord's day by most Christian communities. But does that really make it our Lord Jesus Christ's day? Which Lord was it originally referring to? Before you answer this question, think carefully. The answer might not be the one you were expecting. We need to search the Scriptures before making the suggestion that the Lord in question was our Lord Jesus Christ. But first, following is a brief explanation of the origin of the names of the weekdays as we know them in the English language and their relationship to pagan gods.

Days	Derivation
Sunday	First day of the week: Derived from the Latin *dies solis*, "sun's day," a pagan Roman holiday.
Monday	Second day of the week: Derived from the Anglo-Saxon *monandaeg*, which means "the moon's day." Latin: *dies lunae*, "day of the moon."
Tuesday	Third day of the week: Named for the Norse god of war, Tiu, or Tyr, the son of Odin.
Wednesday	Fourth day of the week: Named to honor Odin, or Woden, chief god in Norse mythology. Onsdag in Sweden and Denmark.
Thursday	Fifth day of the week: Named for Thor, Norse god of thunder. Torsdag in Sweden and Denmark.
Friday	Sixth day of the week: Named for the Norse goddess of love, Frigg, or Frija. Variation of the Old High German *frìatag*, "day of Frija."
Saturday	Seventh day of the week: Named in honor of the Roman god Saturn. Latin: *Saturni*. Sater-daeg by the Anglo-Saxons.

As you can see, each day of the week is named after a pagan god, but our focus will be on the first day of the week, which we have come to know as Sunday.

"The most ancient Germans being pagans and having appropriated their first day of the week to the peculiar adoration of the sun, whereof that day doth yet in our English tongue retain the name of Sunday" (*Verstegan's Antiquities*, p.10). This author is indicating three things to us. First, the word Sunday comes from ancient Germans; second, they were pagans; and third, they dedicated this day to the peculiar worship of their god, the sun.

A Baptist theology professor once said:

> "This word [Sunday] is of heathen origin. It, or a corresponding term in languages and cultures other than Anglo-Saxon, indicates a day dedicated particularly to the worshipful recognition of some deity in the particular pantheon involved. Obviously the exact name indicates the day devoted to the worship of the sun. In pagan use the name, whatever it may be, does not indicate exaltation of this deity above all others, nor exclusive worship of that deity on that day, but only special emphasis on his worship. When in the Roman Empire the sun gained prominence as the symbol of highest divinity this constituted a preparation for the political and ecclesiastical identification of the Lord's Day for Sun-day. . . . With the expansion of Christianity in Europe the day for special Christian worship falling on that of sun worship the name was simply taken over. It has no direct reference to the Hebrew Sabbath. And, of course, there is no close connection between the origin of the name and Christian practice" (William Owen Carver, *Sabbath Observance*, p. 19).

Carver is well aware of the history of this day and therefore makes the declaration clearly, stating that it was taken over from the pagans for political and ecclesiastical gains by the Roman government. Paganism was losing ground to Christianity, so what better way to accommodate both sides then to have the same holy day.

Yet, sun worship has been around since ancient times. The Egyptians worshipped the sun under the name of Ra; the Phoenicians worshipped the sun under the name of Baal; the Chaldeans worshipped the sun under the name of Tammuz; the Greeks worshipped the sun under the name of Apollo, which was later changed to Helios; and the Persians worshipped the sun under the name of Mithras, which finally became *Sol Deus Invictus* (the invisible sun-god) among the Romans. These are just a few of the names given to the sun among ancient pagan societies. Almost all of the civilizations with a recorded history have had a sun-god. The most important thing to notice is that the first day of the week was the day devoted to this deity. These were pre-Christian religions.

One author says, "The ancient peoples of both Old and New World were charmed by it [the sun], as is abundantly revealed by the literature and archaeological remains preserved from the civilizations of the past" (Robert L. Odom, *Sunday in Roman Paganism*, p. 125).

There should not be any doubt to us that the first day of the week was devoted to the worship of the sun, but why do Christians refer to Sunday as the Lord's day? Is it because of Jesus or the sun? I already mentioned that during the Roman Empire Christianity was gaining ground in society and pagans were becoming the minority. The Roman Emperor Constantine was a pagan, but he wanted the support of the Christians, so he passed the venerable day of the sun law in the year AD 321.[1]

I am well aware that Sunday advocates will say that today's Christians refer to Sunday as the Lord's day because Jesus' resurrection took place on the first day of the week, but did you know that Sunday was already referred to as the Lord's day long before Christianity? In the Chaldean's hymns to the sun, the following words are found: "Lord," "Great Lord," "Lord, Light of the legions

---

[1]   Footnote by Philip Schaff, *History of the Christian Church* p. 380.

of the heavens, sun, o Judge!" "The Lord of living beings," and "Lord, illuminator of darkness" (Society of Biblical Archaeology, *Records of the Past*, vol. 11, pp. 123-128).

Some authors have made it even clearer that Sunday was called the Lord's day before Christian times. A Portuguese author says, "The first day of each week, Sunday, was consecrated to Mithra since times remote, as several authors affirm. Because the sun was god, the Lord *par excellence*, Sunday came to be called the Lord's day, as later was done by Christianity" (Agostinho de Almeida Paiva, *O Mitraismo*, p. 3).

This same author compares Mithraism with Sunday-keeping Christianity by saying, "The one and the other celebrated the birth of its god on the 25th of December; and it's beyond doubt that Mithraism preceded Christianity in this and in other points" (Ibid., p. 60).

A historian named Arthur Weigall says, "As a solar festival, Sunday was the sacred day of Mithra; and it is interesting to notice that since Mithra was addressed as Dominus 'Lord,' Sunday must have been 'the Lord's day' long before Christian times" (*The Paganism in Our Christianity*, p. 145).

It is interesting that even non-religious scholars agree that Christianity copied paganism in many aspects, especially that of sun worship, and by calling the first day of the week the Lord's day, something that the pagans did centuries before Christianity. Of course, there were still Christians who were worshipping God just as Jesus taught while on earth, and there still are these Christians today.

Christmas

Sun worshippers had a winter solstice festival on December 25, on which they celebrated Mithra's birthday. Mithra was the sun god of the Persians and later the Romans. The Catholic Church—more specifically Pope Julius I—chose December 25 to celebrate Jesus' birthday.

"It is commonly believed that the church chose this date in an effort to adopt and absorb the traditions of the pagan Saturnalia festival" ("Saturnalia," The History Channel). Those Christian groups that believe they are celebrating Jesus' birthday on December 25 are actually celebrating the sun god Mithra's birthday.

Easter Sunday

Easter Sunday is the most important feast of the year among Christian communities, for Protestants and Catholics alike. Many believe that Easter is of Christian origin, citing Acts 12:4 in the Bible, but the word Easter used here, mainly in the King James Version, is a mistranslation; it should be Passover.

Sunday worship is simply a weekly commemoration of the pagan feast known today as Easter, in which the pagans worshipped the goddess of spring and fertility. Since the Roman Church adopted the sun festival, they had to incorporate all other rituals related to it.

"The Christian festival of Easter incorporates many pagan, or pre-Christian, traditions. The origin of its name is unknown. Scholars believe that it probably comes from *Eastre*, the Anglo-Saxon name of a Germanic goddess of spring and fertility" ("Easter," in Microsoft® Encarta® Online Encyclopedia 2008).

Today's Christians celebrate Easter Sunday thinking that they are doing something that is of Christian origin, but this is far from the truth. What do rabbits and eggs have to do with Jesus? Nothing at all!

The Encarta encyclopedia says the following concerning rabbits and eggs: "Traditions associated with her [goddess *Eastre*] festival survive today in the Easter rabbit, a symbol of fertility, and in colored Easter eggs. Eggs were originally painted with bright colors to represent the sunlight of spring" (Ibid.). Notice that it says that they painted the eggs to represent the sunlight of spring—once again connecting rituals to sun worship!

Almost all theologians today agree that Sunday and Easter are pagan in origin and come from some form of sun worship. A Catholic official made the following declaration:

"The church took the pagan philosophy and made it the buckler of faith against the heathen. She took the pagan, Roman Pantheon, temple of all the gods, and made it sacred to all the martyrs; so it stands to this day. She took the pagan Sunday and made it the Christian Sunday. She took the pagan Easter and made it the feast we celebrate during this season.

Sunday and Easter day are, if we consider their derivation, much the same. In truth, all Sundays are Sundays only because they are a weekly, partial recurrence of Easter day. The pagan Sunday was, in a manner, an unconscious preparation for Easter day. The Sun was a foremost god with heathendom. . . . Hence the church in these countries would seem to have said, 'Keep that old, pagan name. It shall remain consecrated, sanctified.' And thus the pagan Sunday, dedicated to Balder, became the Christian Sunday, sacred to Jesus. The sun is a fitting emblem of Jesus. The Fathers often compared Jesus to the sun; as they compared Mary to the moon, the beautiful moon, the beautiful Mary, shedding her mild, beneficent light on the darkness and night of this world—not light of her own; no Catholic says this; but—light reflected from the sun, Jesus" (William L. Gildea, "Paschale Gaudium," in *The Catholic World*, March 1894, p. 809).

Dear friend, we are called to obey God above man, and God does not share His glory. A Christian pastor once said the following regarding Easter: "The name Easter was adopted from the heathen. It is of Saxon origin, and imports a goddess of the Saxons, or rather of the East, Estera, whose festival was celebrated in the spring of the year, about the Passover season" (Charles Taze Russell, *The New Creation*). p.479

This author even acknowledges the fact that the Roman Church fixed the date so that there would be no confusion among the people between the Passover and the Easter celebration.

He said, "The Ecumenical council of Nice decreed that thenceforth Easter should be celebrated on the Friday following the first full moon after the spring equinox" (Ibid.). P.480

Charles Taze Russell was the founder of the Jehovah's Witness Church, a Christian denomination. He goes on saying that even though Easter is of pagan origin, we Christians need to remember Jesus' death and resurrection on this holyday. He said, "Yea, we would be quite willing to preach Christ in a heathen temple and on a heathen holy day, but would not consider that in so doing we were indorsing either the heathen doctrines or the heathen holy day" (Ibid.). p.382

Most ministers say that even though Sunday worship is of pagan origin, in today's society, we worship Jesus. God established the way in which He wants us to adore Him, and He does not want it mingled with Satan's pagan worship. God says, "the seventh day is the Sabbath of the LORD thy God." God's Sabbath is the seventh day. If Sunday is your sabbath, who is your god? Remember, Sunday and Easter come from paganism—sun worship! Do you want to obey God or the pagan gods?

But, how did sun worship enter the Christian church? I will cover that in the next section.

The Christian Church

During Jesus' time, the Roman Empire had control over the known world, and the Jewish nation was under their dominion. Jesus established His church in Jerusalem, not in Rome as some might think. However, after Jesus' death, His apostles spread the gospel throughout the known world, including Rome, which was considered to be the capital of the world at the time. After the apostles died, many false Christians infiltrated the church with false doctrines, as prophesied by the apostle Paul:

"I know that after my departure fierce wolves will come in among you, not sparing the flock; and from among your own selves will arise men speaking twisted things, to draw away the disciples after them" (Acts 20:29-30).

Just as Paul prophesied, men started teaching twisted things right after his death. One of them was the doctrine of sun worship (held on the first day of the week) as a Christian holy day. Paganism was the Roman Empire's official religion, and the sun was the most important god of the Greco-Roman pantheon.

Franz Cumont makes note of this:

> "Solar pantheism, which grew up among the Syrians of the Hellenistic period as a result of the influence of Chaldean astrolatry, imposed itself upon the whole Roman world under the empire... That theological system shows incidentally the last form assumed by the pagan idea of God. In this matter Syria was Rome's teacher and predecessor. The last formula reached by the religion of the pagan Semites and in consequence by that of the Romans, was a divinity unique, almighty, eternal, universal and ineffable that revealed itself throughout nature, but whose most splendid and most energetic manifestation was the sun" (Franz Cumont, *The Oriental Religions in Roman Paganism*, p. 134).

It is well documented that the Romans worshipped the sun, as another author says, "This solar faith was the culmination of Hellenistic-Oriental and Roman Paganism. It was the vitalizing power in pagan theology and afforded the most convincing symbol of that light which was the aim of philosophy and religion. It was the source of a mystical devotion in which peasant and philosopher could participate" (S. Angus, *The Religious Quests of the Graeco-Roman World*, p. 276).

Remember, Jesus established His church in Jerusalem, and the first Christians were of Hebrew origin. They had the knowledge of the true Sabbath, the seventh day of the week. This gives no room for the pagan sun worship doctrine to enter through them, so it had to have been the gentiles of pagan background who introduced this false doctrine after the apostles had died, especially Paul.

Roman Week Days

We already know that during Jesus' days the Roman Empire was in the dominion of the known world, and that the Romans were pagans. They had named each day of the week after one of the seven visible celestial bodies, dedicating each day to one of those bodies in order to honor them.

The table below presents the days of the week, their names and Latin meanings.

Dies	Dies	Dies	Dies	Dies	Dies	Dies
Solis	Lunae	Martis	Mercurii	Jovis	Veneris	Saturni
(day of the sun)	(day of the moon)	(day of mars)	(day of mercury)	(day of jupiter)	(day of venus)	(day of saturn)

During the time of the apostles, these were the names by which the Romans called their days. Some Christians suggest that the apostles kept Sunday, and others go as far as suggesting that even Paul kept Sunday as the Lord's day. However, was not Paul a Roman citizen? Therefore, Paul would have known that the first day of the week was dedicated to the sun god and called *dies solis*, "day of the sun." As a follower of Christ, he worshipped the Lord on Sabbath, not Sunday, a day dedicated to the sun god. Satan wants to deceive the world. However, we can avoid his ploys by studying the Bible. For Jesus said, "You search the Scriptures because you think that in them you have eternal life; and it is they that bear witness about me" (John 5:39).

WHAT ABOUT EARLY CHRISTIAN WRITINGS?

Since there is no biblical support for Sunday as the new Christian Sabbath, those Christians advocating for Sunday as the Sabbath have to quote other writings besides the Bible that support this theory. The authors who support Sunday worship are going directly against what the Holy Scriptures teach, since there is no biblical evidence for a Sunday Sabbath.

In the following section, I will review some of the most popular sources used as evidence for Sunday worship among Christians. To unmask false doctrines, it is necessary to study them so that we are not deceived by Satan's lies.

The Fathers of the Roman Catholic Church

Today's Christians quote from the church fathers or the early Christians when they delve into the subject of the Sabbath. Yet, the people who are quoted as church fathers or early Christians were not what they are portrayed to be, since the original church father was Jesus. We might consider the apostles to be church fathers, and the early Christians were those who accepted the gospel of Jesus during those days. However, based on their philosophies, the so-called "church fathers" are the fathers of the Roman Catholic Church, which should not to be confused with the church that Jesus established. Let us take a look at some of these people and some of the books that are thought to come from the early church.

Ignatius of Antioch

"Ignatius of Antioch, also called Theophorus (ho Theophoros), was born in Syria, around the year 50; died at Rome between AD 98 and 117" ("St. Ignatius of Antioch," in *The Catholic Encyclopedia*).

51

Ignatius is often quoted by Sunday keepers as proof that the early church kept Sunday as the Sabbath after Christ's death. "Be not seduced by strange doctrines nor by antiquated fables, which are profitless. For if even unto this day we live after the manner of Judaism, we avow that we have not received grace. . . . If then those who had walked in ancient practices attained unto newness of hope, no longer observing Sabbaths but fashioning their lives after the Lord's day, on which our life also arose through Him and through His death which some men deny . . . how shall we be able to live apart from Him? . . . It is monstrous to talk of Jesus Christ and to practice Judaism. For Christianity did not believe in Judaism, but Judaism in Christianity" (J. B. Lightfoot, "Ignatius to the Magnesians," in *The Apostolic Fathers*, chap. 8:1, 9:1-2, 10:3).

According to tradition, Ignatius was one of the children Jesus took in His arms and blessed. However, this claim is not possible—Jesus died in the year AD 31, and Ignatius was born around AD 50. Furthermore, his letters cannot be considered as proof, because there were many spurious ones. *The Catholic Encyclopedia* says the following: "We find these seven mentioned not only by Eusebius ("Hist. eccl.", III, xxxvi) but also by St. Jerome (De viris illust., c. xvi). Of later collections of Ignatian letters which have been preserved, the oldest is known as the "long recension." This collection, the author of which is unknown, dates from the latter part of the fourth century. It contains the seven genuine and six spurious letters, but even the genuine epistles were greatly interpolated to lend weight to the personal views of its author. For this reason they are incapable of bearing witness to the original form. The spurious letters in this recension are those that purport to be from Ignatius" ("St. Ignatius of Antioch").

The Catholic scholar that wrote this article declares that Ignatius' letters cannot be used as a witness since they are not in their original form; therefore, it is not clear if he actually wrote about Sunday as the new Christian Sabbath or not. Even if he did, it does not overrule the authority of the Bible, much less that of Jesus.

Justin Martyr

Justin Martyr is another person often quoted as part of early Christian literature in support of Sunday worship. So who was Justin Martyr? *The Catholic Encyclopedia* describes him as follows: "Christian apologist, born at Flavia Neapolis, about AD 100, converted to Christianity about AD 130, taught and defended the Christian religion in Asia Minor and at Rome, where he suffered martyrdom about the year 165" ("St. Justin Martyr").

He was born in a Greek pagan family, and as a pagan, we can safely assume that he worshipped the sun at some point. One of his quotes, which is often used by today's Christians, is as follows: "But Sunday is the day on which we all hold our common assembly, because it is the first day on which God, having wrought a change in the darkness and matter, made the world; and Jesus Christ our Saviour on the same day rose from the dead" ("Weekly Worship of the Christians," in *First Apology of St. Justin Martyr*, chap. LXVII).

Again, we have to keep in mind that he was raised as a pagan, a sun worshipper. He knew that the first day of the week was dedicated to the sun among the pagans. For he declared, "For He was crucified on the day before that of Saturn (Saturday); and on the day after that of Saturn, which is the day of the Sun [Sunday], having appeared to His apostles and disciples, He taught them these things, which we have submitted to you also for your consideration" (Ibid.).

Based on his upbringing, I believe that Justin Martyr was a sun-worshipper and continued being a sun-worshipper after he accepted Jesus, only pretending to be celebrating Christ's resurrection. He was a philosopher[1]

---

[1]   Edward Backhouse and Charles Tylor, *Early Church History, to the Death of Constantine*, p. 56.

before he settled in Rome as a Christian teacher, but he continued to wear the philosopher's mantle[2] even after he had accepted the new Christian religion. How can a professed Christian continue wearing the philosopher's mantle? He was now a Christian philosopher. Is there such a thing? No. The new Christian religion was spreading rapidly and paganism was losing ground; therefore, I believe this agile philosopher went with the crowd as a new convert, continuing his career as a philosopher and not going against what was now the majority. This is called politics, my friend.

Tertullian

Quintus Septimius Florens Tertullianus, anglicized as Tertullian, is believed to have lived from AD 155 to 222 and was raised in Carthage as a pagan. In one of his writings, he is quoted as saying, "Therefore, since God originated Adam uncircumcised and unobservant of the Sabbath, consequently his offspring also, Abel, offering him sacrifices, uncircumcised and unobservant of the Sabbath, was by Him commended" (*An Answer to the Jews*, chap. 2).

My first question regarding this quote is how does he know if Adam was or was not circumcised? One can only assume that he was not. Second, Adam was created on the sixth day, and God rested on the seventh day. How can Tertullian say that Adam was unobservant of the Sabbath? If God observed the Sabbath, why would Adam not do the same? If God rested on the seventh day, would one not think that Adam would imitate God? In my mind, it is obvious that Adam kept the Sabbath.

Later in life Tertullian adopted views that came to be regarded as heretical. This is another example of a pagan who converted to Christianity, no later than AD 197,[3] and tried to teach the gospel of Christ, which he obviously did

---

2   Ibid., p. 60.
3   "Tertullian," in *The Catholic Encyclopedia*.

not comprehend. Tertullian spent most of his life as a pagan, teaching a new doctrine to the Christians, a dogma he practiced as a pagan—sun worship.

Polycarp Bishop of Smyrna

When Sunday-keeping advocates quote these so-called fathers of the Christian church, they hardly ever mention Polycarp. Is this because they know that he kept the true Sabbath? It is believed that he lived from AD 69 to 155.[4] Polycarp was the bishop of the church in Smyrna, which was located in Asia Minor—the single church within the Christian communities that taught and kept the true Sabbath. The other churches kept Sunday as the Lord's day. Polycarp was also the only bishop with a direct connection to the apostles. It is believed that he was a disciple of the apostle John.[5] No wonder he was the only one keeping the true Sabbath!

There is other evidence that Polycarp kept the true Sabbath, one of them being that he endorsed the commandments of God, and the Sabbath is the fourth commandment. Here is one statement from Polycarp in his letter to the Philippians: "Now He that raised Him from the dead will raise us also; if we do His will and walk in His commandments and love the things which He loved, abstaining from all unrighteousness, covetousness, love of money, evil speaking, false witness; not rendering evil for evil or railing for railing or blow for blow or cursing for cursing" (J. B. Lightfoot, "Polycarp," in *The Apostolic Fathers*, chap. 2:2).

Another piece of evidence that shows that Polycarp and the church of Smyrna kept the seventh-day Sabbath was that Polycarp opposed the change in the date of the Passover to Sunday, whereas Sunday observers accepted this change. "The visit of St. Polycarp to Rome is described by St. Irenæus in a letter to Pope Victor written under the

---

4   "Polycarp," in *The Catholic Encyclopedia*.

5   Charles Tilstone Beke, *Jesus the Messiah*, p. 226.

following circumstances. The Asiatic Christians differed from the rest of the Church in their manner of observing Easter. While the other Churches kept the feast on a Sunday, the Asiatics celebrated it on the 14th of Nisan, whatever day of the week this might fall on" ("Polycarp" in *The Catholic Encyclopedia*).

This is very interesting. While some Christian churches were celebrating the pagan tradition of Easter Sunday, which has nothing to do with Christ, others were remembering Christ's death on the Jewish Passover, which was celebrated on the 14th of Nisan.

The pagans disguised as Christians did not want to be accused of celebrating the Jewish Passover; therefore, Constantine made the official change in AD 325. "Accordingly, by the solemn decree of the pagan Emperor [Constantine] in his Council of Nicaea, AD 325, the Friday before Easter Sunday was declared to be the day of the Christian Passover, and not the fourteenth of the month Nisan" (Charles Tilstone Beke, *Jesus the Messiah*, p. 226).

If Constantine had not made this change, the Christian feast known today as Easter would fall on the same day as the Jewish feast of Passover, on the 14th of Nisan, which could fall on any day of the week. Easter is really the feast of the goddess Eastre; however, because the so-called Christians did not want to be accused of paganism, they disguised it under the Christian mantel.

You might be asking yourself what this has to do with anything. Let me explain my point. In order to conflate the death of Christ and the pagan feast known as Easter, the Friday before Easter Sunday has to be the Friday on which Jesus died on the cross so that Christ's resurrection can be celebrated on Easter Sunday. If Christians celebrated His death on the 14th of Nisan, which could fall on any day, then there would not be a way for the pagan feast of Easter Sunday to be disguised as a Christian holy day.

Polycarp understood this, and therefore, he opposed the change. Polycarp's martyrdom is described in a letter from the church of Smyrna as follows: "But when at length he brought his prayer to an end, after remembering all who at any time had come in his way, small and great, high and low, and all the universal Church throughout the world, the hour of departure being come, they seated him (Polycarp) on an ass and brought him into the city, it being a high Sabbath" (J. B. Lightfoot, *The Apostolic Fathers*, p. 205). "Now the blessed Polycarp was martyred on the second day of the first part of the month *Xanthicus*, on the seventh before the *kalends* of March, on a great Sabbath, at the eight hour" (Ibid., p. 210).

There is further evidence that Polycarp's followers kept the Sabbath. The seventeenth-century historian William Cave reported that the early Christians in Asia Minor (which he called "the Eastern parts") kept the Sabbath. He says the following:

> ". . . the Sabbath or Saturday (for so the word sabbatum is constantly used in the writings of the fathers, when speaking of it as it relates to Christians) was held by them in great veneration, and especially in the Eastern parts honoured with all the public solemnities of religion. . . . This is plain, not only from some passages in Ignatius and Clemens's Constitutions, but from writers of more unquestionable credit and authority. Athanasius, bishop of Alexandria, tells us, that they assembled on Saturdays, not that they were infected with Judaism, but only to worship Jesus Christ, the Lord of the Sabbath." (*Primitive Christianity: or the Religion of the Ancient Christians in the First Ages of the Gospel*, pp. 84-85).

Epistle of Barnabas

Another source often used as evidence of early Christian literature for pro-Sunday keeping is the letter of Barnabas.

The letter of Barnabas is said to have been written around the beginning of the second century. In it we can find the following quote: "I will make the beginning of the eighth day which is the beginning of another world" (J. B. Lightfoot, "Epistle of Barnabas," in *The Apostolic Fathers*, chap. 15:8). This eighth day is Sunday, the beginning of another world under Jesus. Sounds convincing, doesn't it? Many people have been fooled by this forgery. There is no such thing as an eighth-day doctrine in the Bible; this was not written by the Barnabas mentioned in the Bible.

Most scholars do not recognize the epistle of Barnabas as a legitimate source. "By far the greater numbers of theologians deny that it was written by Barnabas; and really its contents are of such a nature that it would be very hard to reconcile them to his authorship. The author takes such a hostile position toward the Old Testament as could scarcely be conceived of by an apostle. He teaches that the Old Testament has never been of any force" (Benedict Welte and Heinrich Joseph Wetzer, "Barnabas," in *Wetzer and Welte's Kirchenlexikon*).

The Catholic Encyclopedia states the following: "About the year AD 200, even in Alexandria the Epistle of Barnabas was not regarded by everyone as an inspired writing" ("Epistle of Barnabas"). Another author says the following about the epistle of Barnabas: "It is a treatise of little value, and abounds in allegorical interpretations of the Old Testament, more ingenious than rational" (Edward Backhouse and Charles Tylor, *Early Church History, to the Death of Constantine*, p. 65).

The epistle of Barnabas does not have any credibility, thus it confuses the church, but only those who want to be confused will let themselves be confused, because the Scriptures are clear—the seventh day is the Sabbath day.

The Didache

"But every Lord's day . . . gather yourselves together and break bread, and give thanksgiving after having confessed your transgressions, that your sacrifice may be pure. But let no one that is at variance with his fellow come together with you, until they be reconciled, that your sacrifice may not be profaned" (J. B. Lightfoot, "Didache," in *The Apostolic Fathers*, chap. 14).

So, what is the Didache, and who wrote it? Some claim that it is the doctrines of the apostles, but it is not. Indeed, it is nowhere near the apostles! *The Catholic Encyclopedia* states: "A short treatise which was accounted by some of the Fathers as next to Holy Scripture. It was rediscovered in 1873 by Bryennios, Greek Orthodox metropolitan of Nicomedia, in the codex from which, in 1875, he had published the full text of the Epistles of St. Clement" ("The Didache").

Jonathan A. Draper writes about its date of composition: "Few scholars now date the text later than the end of the first century CE or the first few decades of the second" (*The Apostolic Fathers: the Didache, Expository Times*, vol. 117, no. 5, p. 178).

Draper, in another of his works, makes the following declaration: "Since it was rediscovered in a monastic library in Constantinople and published by P. Bryennios in 1883, the Didache or Teaching of the Twelve Apostles has continued to be one of the most disputed of early Christian texts. It has been depicted by scholars as anything between the original of the Apostolic Decree (c. 50 C.E.) and a late archaizing fiction of the early third century. It bears no date itself, nor does it make reference to any datable external event" (*The Didache in Modern Research*, p. 72).

Scholars do not believe it was written by the apostles. However, people often quote from it as if it was. Instead of quoting human works, we must turn to the Bible, which was inspired by the Holy Spirit, for truth regarding doctrinal issues.

The Didascalia Apostolorum

The *Didascalia*, also known as the Apostolic Constitutions, is a series of books that are believed to have been apostolic but are not. *"Didascalia Apostolorum*, a treatise which pretends to have been written by the Apostles at the time of the Council of Jerusalem (Acts, xv), but is really a composition of the third century. It was first published in 1854, in Syriac" ("Didascalia Apostolorum," in *The Original Catholic Encyclopedia*).

Philip Schaff wrote, "It is, in form, a literary fiction, professing to be a bequest of all the apostles, handed down through the Roman Bishop Clement, or dictated to him." "The first six books which have strongly Jewish-Christian tone, were composed, with the exception of some later interpolations, at the end of the third century, in Syria. The seventh book is an expansion of the Didache. . . . The second Trullan council of 692 rejected it for its heretical interpolations" (*History of the Christian Church*, vol. 2, pp. 185-186).

The *Didascalia Apostolorum* is founded upon the *Didache*,[6] and like the *Didache*, it was written as though by the apostles. Today's Christians quote this document as if it was a legitimate source written by the apostles, but it is clearly not.

Following are two quotes that people use to prove that the Lord's day is Sunday: "But from the eve of the fifth day till cock-crowing break your fast when it is daybreak of the first day of the week, which is the Lord's day" (*Didascalia*, bk. V, sec. III), and "On the day of our Lord's resurrection, which is the Lord's day, meet more diligently, sending praise to God that made the universe by Jesus, and sent Him to us, and condescended to let

---

6   "The Didache" in *The Catholic Encyclopedia*.

Him suffer, and raised Him from the dead" (*Didascalia,* bk. II, sec. VII).

Quotes like these are often used by individuals who want to justify worshipping on Sunday. However, the Bible and only the Bible should be used as the ultimate source for truth and for our salvation. If the Bible has all the answers, why should we search anywhere else? But those individuals who want to teach that Sunday is the Sabbath, they have to search other writings since there is no Biblical evidence for this teaching.

Many Christians in the fourth century were still keeping the true Sabbath; therefore, the church organized the Council of Laodicea to pass a rule stating that the Sabbath was no longer to be kept holy and that Sunday would be observed as the Lord's day. "Christians should not Judaize and should not be idle on the Sabbath, but should work on that day; they should, however, particularly reverence the Lord's day and, if possible, not work on it, because they were Christians" (*Council of Laodicea,* canon 29).

When individuals site these uninspired writings, also known as early Christian writings, they are trying to prove that Christians no longer need to keep the Sabbath but should keep Sunday, which they refer to as the Lord's day. They think that they are obeying God by following a tradition that they believe was started by the apostles. However, the Bible and many theologians prove otherwise. It was the Roman Catholic Church that established these traditions. Even if the apostles had begun teaching Sunday worship—which they did not!—Jesus never taught that Sunday should replace the Sabbath during his lifetime or in the future.

Paul said the following: "I marvel that ye are so soon removed from him that called you into the grace of Christ unto another gospel: Which is not another; but there be some that trouble you, and would pervert the gospel of Christ. But though we, or an angel from heaven, preach any other gospel unto you than that which we have preached unto you, let him be accursed. As we said before, so say I now again, if any man preach any other gospel unto you than that ye have received, let him be accursed" (Galatians 1:6-9, KJV).

If anyone, even the apostles, preaches any other gospel other than the one of Jesus, let him be accursed. All of the early Christian writings proclaiming Sunday as the replacement for the Sabbath are accursed according to the Holy Scriptures. We must obey God and keep His Ten Commandments, instead of looking to man for guidance.

Formation of the Roman Catholic Church

Many of the Christians after the first century were pagan converts and had little or no guidance from the true gospel of Christ; therefore, many of their pagan beliefs were used as part of their worship. Gordon Laing writes:

"Cults of the sun, as we know from many sources, had attained great vogue during the second, third, and fourth centuries. Sun-worshippers indeed formed one of the big groups in that religious world in which Christianity was fighting for a place. Many of them became converts to Christianity and in all probability carried into their new religion some remnants of their old beliefs. The complaint of Pope Leo in the fifth century that worshippers in St. Peter's turned away from the altar and faced the door so that they could adore the rising sun is not without its significance in regard to the number of Christians who at one time had been adherents of some form of sun-worship. It is of course impossible to say precisely in what way their influence manifested itself. We do know, however, of analogues between Christ and the sun; he was designated the Sun of Righteousness; and our Christmas falls on the date of the festival of a popular sun-god in Rome." (*Survivals of Roman Religion*, p. 192).

These pagan converts continued with some of the remnants of paganism such that others accused them of being idolaters and charged them of worshipping the sun, among other things. Tertullian responded to the accusation of worshipping the sun: "The Christians of those times did generally pray towards the east and the sun-rising, which the heathens themselves also did, though upon different grounds: and partly because they performed the solemnities of their religion upon the day that was dedicated to the sun" (*Primitive Christianity: or the Religion of the Ancient Christians in the First Ages of the Gospel*, p. 85).

Did Christ pray to the east? Of course not! But not only that, these pagan converts also built their churches facing the east! "They [the churches] were generally built towards the east, (towards which they performed the more solemn parts of their worship)" (Ibid., p. 97).

Tertullian's excuse was that the east was the representation of Christ.[7] One author shows how extensive the Christian worship toward the east was: "Christians prayed to the east, as the type of Christ, the Sun of Righteousness (Clem.Al.Strom. vii, 7, p. 856; Damas. iv, 12), whence also in baptism they turned to the east to confess Christ (S.Jer.in Am. vi, 14. Ambros.de iis que initiantur c,2), and their churches were toward the east (Tert. c. Valent. C. 3. Const. Ap. ii, 57), so that other positions were rare exceptions" (C. Dodgson, *Tertullian*, vol. 1, p. 38).

The claim that the early Christians kept Sunday as their Sabbath has no basis, as we have already discussed. However, the new converts knew the difference between the true Sabbath and the first day of the week, as one historian writes: "The Christians in the ancient church very soon distinguished the first day of the week, Sunday; however, not as a Sabbath, but as an assembly day of the church, to study the Word of God together and to celebrate the ordinances one with another: without a shadow

---

7   Ibid., p. 98.

of doubt this took place as early as the first part of the second century" (*Geschichte des Sonntags*, p. 60).

Another author says: "The weekly commemoration of the resurrection supplemented, but did not supersede, the ancient Sabbath" (Edward Backhouse and Charles Tylor, *Early Church History, to the Death of Constantine*, p. 104). Many Christian communities existed during those days, but one rose above all when Constantine became emperor of Rome. Constantine worshipped the sun, as Philip Schaff says, "At first Constantine, like his father, in the spirit of the Neo-Platonic syncretism of dying heathendom, reverenced all the gods as mysterious powers; especially Apollo, the god of the sun" (*History of the Christian Church*, p. 14).

Constantine established Christianity as the official religion of the empire and applied the predicate "Catholic" to the church in all official documents (Ibid., p. 13). Schaff also said, "The Constantinian toleration was a temporary measure of state policy, which, as indeed the edict expressly states the motive, promised the greatest security to the public peace and the protection of all divine and heavenly powers, for emperor and empire. It was, as the result teaches, but the necessary transition step to a new order of things. It opened the door to the elevation of Christianity, and specifically of Catholic hierarchical Christianity, with its exclusiveness towards heretical and schismatic sects, to be the religion of the state" (Ibid., p. 30).

At this time in history, the Roman Catholic Church rose as an institution. Before Christianity, paganism was the official religion of the state, and the worship of the sun was part of the service. Alonzo T. Jones writes: "The worship of the sun itself was the principal worship of the Romans in the time of Constantine. The sun, as represented in Apollo, was the chief and patron divinity recognized by Augustus" (*The Two Republics*, p. 196). Jones further declared that "in the time of Constantine, and in Constantine himself, the worship of the sun occupied the imperial seat, and was the imperial religion of Rome" (Ibid., p. 202).

During Constantine's reign, Christianity came to be the new religion of the state and its official church was the Roman Catholic Church. The church had control of the empire and paganism was overtaken, but many of the customs of paganism that could not be suppressed were transferred to Christianity. At this time, Sunday officially became the Christian day of rest.

Arthur Weigall made the following declaration: "It seems more likely in fact, that they [Christians] were influenced here, as in so many other matters, by pagan custom, and that Sunday came to be celebrated because the Mithraists and other sun-worshippers regarded it as a sacred holiday, and the habit could not be suppressed" (*The Paganism in Our Christianity*, p. 236). Weigall also wrote, "When the Church had become a State institution, however, the need of holy days and festivals began to be felt, and indeed, it was essential to give a Christian significance to those of pagan origin which could not be suppressed" (Ibid., p. 228).

This historian indicates without a doubt that Sunday was instituted as a Christian holy day when the church became a state institution in the fourth century. Prior to this declaration, we know that false Christians after the apostles were also Sunday keepers—not by command of Christ or of the apostles, but by their own pagan ideology.

As the Roman Catholic Church emerged, Constantine became the first pope. Many people will contest this fact, but there are many reasons why he was, in fact, the first pope. First, he was the person who established the church as an institution in the empire. Second, he was the pontifex maximus; the pope is also referred to as such because the Roman Catholic Church adopted the title, which is of pagan origin, when they took over the Roman Empire. One author stated: "Paganism had its pontifex maximus, which was applied to the deified Roman emperors from the days of Caligula" (John Nevins Andrews, *History of the Sabbath and First Day of the Week*, p. 316).

Finally, Constantine summoned the first council ever, known as the Council of Nicaea, and we know today that only the pope can summon a council. Schaff says, "In the year 325, as patron of the church, he summoned the council of Nicaea" (*History of the Christian Church*, p. 32). Schaff also says, "And as his predecessors were supreme pontiffs of the heathen religion of the empire, so he desired to be looked upon as a sort of bishop, as universal bishop of the external affairs of the church" (Ibid., p. 13).

The Catholic Church, established by Constantine, was and is the Roman's pagan religion disguised as Christianity. Is not Latin the official language of the Catholic Church? Latin was the official language of Rome—but Christianity originated in Jerusalem, not in Rome.

FIRST SUNDAY LAW

Constantine as the universal bishop of the Roman Catholic Church passed the edict of *dies solis*, the "day of the sun," in AD 321. "On the venerable Day of the Sun let the magistrates and people residing in cities rest, and let all workshops be closed. In the country, however, persons engaged in agriculture may freely and lawfully continue their pursuits; because it often happens that another day is not so suitable for grain-sowing or for vine-planting; lest by neglecting the proper moment for such operations the bounty of heaven should be lost." (Philip Schaff, *History of the Christian Church*, p. 380, footnote 1).

This is how Sunday officially became the holy day for Christians—not by God's command, but by Pope Constantine, the universal bishop of the Roman Catholic Church. The word "Catholic" comes from the Greek word *katholikos*, which means "universal"; this clearly makes Constantine the first Catholic pope! Based on our research, it is clear that Peter was not the first pope, Jesus did not establish the Catholic Church, and Sunday keeping is not of Christian origin. Arthur Weigall says this about Sunday: "The refusal of certain people to work or to play on Sundays owing to religious scruples is evidence of so un-Christian and so gross a superstition that the mind of the thinking man is staggered by it" (*Paganism in Our Christianity*, p. 238).

Please do not think that I am trying to attack anyone or any denomination or to produce hatred; all I am trying to do is to show people "the great prostitute who is seated on many waters, with whom the kings of the earth have committed sexual immorality, and with the wine of whose sexual immorality the dwellers on earth have become drunk" (Revelation 17:1-2). The whole world is drunk with her false doctrines. "Babylon the great, mother of prostitutes and of earth's abominations. And I saw the woman, drunk with the blood of the saints, the blood of the martyrs of Jesus" (verses 5-6).

The Bible identifies the Roman Catholic Church as Babylon, and her daughters as those Protestant churches that teach the same false doctrines as their mother, especially the Sunday doctrine. They have made the earth full of abominations. They are planning to institute a latter Sunday law, which I will cover later in this book. Most Protestants today do not know or do not want to accept the true Sabbath, so they willingly deny these facts. They want to keep the spurious Sabbath, Sunday. The Roman Catholic Church changed the Sabbath from the seventh day of the week to the first, but Protestants do not want to admit it. The Roman Catholic Church has challenged the Protestants to show proof of a change with the Bible only, since Protestants claim that it is the sole teacher—"the Bible and the Bible only," as they say. Let us take a look at Rome's challenge.

ROME'S CHALLENGE TO PROTESTANTS

The following text was taken from *The Clifton Tracts,* vol. 4, which was written by the Brotherhood of St. Vincent of Paul, a Roman Catholic source, and printed as early as 1854. The essay is geared toward Protestants and is titled "Why Don't You Keep Holy the Sabbath-Day?"

"I am going to propose a very plain and serious question, to which I would entreat all who profess to follow 'the Bible and the Bible only' to give their most earnest attention. It is this: Why do you not keep holy the Sabbath-day? The command of Almighty God stands clearly written in the Bible in these words: 'Remember the Sabbath-day, to keep it holy. Six days shalt thou labor, and do all thy work; but the seventh day is the Sabbath of the Lord thy God; in it thou shalt not do any work' (Exod. xx. 8,9) And again, 'Six days shall work be done; but on the seventh day there shall be to you an holy day, a Sabbath of rest to the Lord; whosoever doeth work therein shall be put to death. Ye shall kindle no fire through out your habitations upon the Sabbath day' (Exod. xxxv. 2, 3). How strict and precise is God's commandment upon this head! No work whatever was to be done on the day which He had chosen to set apart for Himself and to make holy; He required of His people that they should not even light a fire upon that day. And accordingly, when the children of Israel 'found a man that gathered sticks upon the Sabbath-day,' 'the Lord said unto Moses, The man shall be surely put to death; all the congregation shall stone him with stones without the camp' (Numbers xv. 35). Such being God's commands then, I ask you again, why do you not obey it? Why do you not keep holy the Sabbath-day?

"You will answer me, perhaps, that you *do* keep holy the Sabbath day; for that you abstain from all the worldly business and diligently go to church, and say your prayers, and read your Bible at home, every Sunday of your lives.

"But *Sunday is not the Sabbath-day*. Sunday is the *first* day of the week; the Sabbath-day was the *seventh* day of the week. Almighty God did not give a commandment that men should keep holy *one day in seven;* but He named His own day, and said distinctly, 'Thou shalt keep holy the *seventh day;'* and he assigned a reason for choosing this day rather than any other - a reason which belongs only to the seventh day of the week, and cannot be applied to the rest. He says, 'For in six days the Lord made the heaven and the earth, the sea and all that in them is, and rested the seventh day; *wherefore* the Lord blessed the Sabbath-day and hallowed it.' Almighty God ordered that all men should rest from their labor on the seventh day, because He too had rested on that day: He did not rest on Sunday, but on Saturday. On Sunday, which is the first day of the week, He *began* the work of creation. He did not finish it; it was on Saturday that He *'ended* His work which He had made; and He rested on the seventh day from all His work which He had made; and God blessed the seventh day, and sanctified it, because that in it He had rested from all His work which God created and made' (Gen. ii. 2, 3) Nothing can be more plain and easy to understand than all this; and there is nobody who attempts to deny it; it is acknowledged by everybody that the day which Almighty God appointed to be kept holy was Saturday, not Sunday. Why do you then keep holy the Sunday, and not Saturday?

"You will tell me that Saturday was the *Jewish* Sabbath, but that the *Christian* Sabbath has been changed to Sunday. Changed! but by whom? Who has the authority to change an express commandment of God? When God has spoken and said, Thou shalt keep holy the seventh day, who shall dare to say, Nay, thou mayest work and do all manner of worldly business on the seventh day; but thou shalt keep holy the first day in its stead? This is a most important question, which I know not how you can answer.

"You are a Protestant, and you profess to go by the Bible and the Bible only; and yet in so important a matter as the observance of one day in seven as a holy day, you go against the plain letter of the Bible, and put another day in the place of that day which the Bible has commanded. The command to keep holy the seventh day is one of the Ten Commandments; you believe that the other nine are still binding; who gave you authority to tamper with the fourth? If you are consistent with your own principles, if you really follow the Bible and the Bible only, you ought to be able to produce some portion of the New Testament in which this fourth commandment is expressly altered, or at least from which you may confidently infer that it was the will of God that Christians should make that change in its observance which you have made. Let us see whether any such passages can be found. I will look for them in the writings of your own champions, who have attempted to defend your practice in this matter.

"1. The first text which I find quoted upon the subject is this: 'Let no man judge you in respect of an holy day, or of the new moon, or of the Sabbath-days' (Col. ii. 16). I could understand a Bible Christian arguing from this passage, that we ought to make no difference between Saturday, Sunday, and every other day of the week; that under the Christian dispensation all such distinctions of days were done away with; one day was as good and as holy as another; there were to be no Sabbaths, no holy days at all. But not one syllable does it say about the obligation of the Sabbath being *transferred* from one day to another.

"2. Secondly, the words of St. John are quoted, 'I was in the Spirit on the Lord's day (Apoc. i. 10). Is it possible that anybody can for a moment imagine that here is a safe and clear rule for changing the weekly feast from the seventh to the first day? This passage is utterly silent upon such a subject; it does but give us Scriptural authority for calling some one day in particular (it does not even say *which* day) 'the Lord's day.'

"3. Next we are reminded that St. Paul bade his Corinthian converts, 'upon the first day of the week, lay by them in store, that there might be no gatherings' when he himself came (1 Cor. xvi. 2). How is this supposed to affect the law of the Jewish Sabbath? It commands a certain act of almsgiving to be done on the first day of the week. It says absolutely nothing about not doing certain other acts of prayer and public worship on the seventh day.

"4. But it was 'on the first day of the week' when the disciples were assembled with closed doors for fear of the Jews, and Jesus stood in the midst of them;

and again, it was eight days afterwards (that is, on the first day of the following week) that 'the disciples were within, and Thomas with them,' and Jesus again came and stood in the midst (John xx. 19, 26): that is to say, it was on the evening of the day of the Resurrection that our Lord first showed Himself to many disciples gathered together; and after eight days He again showed Himself to the same company, with the further addition of St. Thomas. What is there in these facts to do away with the obligation of keeping holy the seventh day? Our Lord rose from dead on the first day of the week, and on the same day at evening He appears to many of His disciples; He appears again on that day [of the] week, and perhaps also on other days in the interval. Let Protestants, if they will, keep holy the first day of the week in grateful commemoration of that stupendous mystery, the Resurrection of Christ, and of the evidence He vouchsafed to give of it to His doubting disciples; but this is no scriptural authority for ceasing to keep holy another day of the week which God had expressly commanded to be kept holy for another and altogether different reason.

"5. But lastly, we have the example of the Apostles themselves. 'Upon the first day of the week, when the disciples came together to break bread, Paul preached unto them, ready to depart on the morrow; and continued his speech until midnight' (Acts xx. 7). Here we have clear proof that the disciples came together for the celebration of the Holy Eucharist, and that they heard a sermon on a Sunday. But is there any proof that they had not done the same on Saturday also? Is it not expressly written concerning those same early Christians, that they 'continued *daily* with one accord in the temple, breaking bread from house to house?' (Acts ii. 46). And as a matter of fact, do we not know from other sources that, in many parts of the Church, the ancient Christians were in the habit of meeting together for public worship, to receive Holy Communion, and to perform the other offices, on Saturdays just the same as on Sundays? Again, then, I say, let Protestants keep holy, if they will, the first day of the week, in order that they may resemble those Christians who were gathered together on that day in the upper chamber in

Troas; but let them remember that this cannot possibly release them from the obligation of keeping holy *another* day which Almighty God has ordered to be kept holy, because on that day He 'rested from all His work'.

"I do not know of any other passages of holy Scripture which Protestants are in the habit of quoting to defend their practice of keeping holy the first day of the week instead of the seventh; yet surely those which I have quoted are not such as should satisfy any reasonable man, who looks upon the written word of God as *they* profess to look upon it, namely as the *one only* appointed means of learning God's will, and who really desires to learn and to obey that will in all things with humbleness and simplicity of heart. It is absolutely impossible that a reasonable and thoughtful person should be satisfied, by the texts that I have quoted, that the almighty God intended the obligation of Saturday under the old law to be transferred to Sunday under the new. And yet Protestants do so transfer it, and never seem to have the slightest misgivings lest, in doing so, they should be guilty of breaking one of God's commandments. Why is this? Because, although they talk so largely about following the Bible and the Bible only, they are really guided in this matter by the voice of tradition. Yes, as much as they may have in fact no other authority to allege for this most important change. The present generation of Protestants keep Sunday holy instead of Saturday, because they received it as part of the Christian religion from the last generation, and that generation received it from the generation before, and so on backwards from one generation to another, by a continual succession, until we come to the time of the (so called) Reformation, when it so happened that those who conducted the change of religion in this country left this particular portion of Catholic faith, and practice untouched.

"But, had it happened otherwise, - had some one or other of the 'Reformers' taken it into his head to denounce the observance of Sunday as a Popish corruption and superstition, and to insist upon it that Saturday was the day which God had appointed to be kept holy, and that He had never authorized the observance of any other - all Protestants would have been obliged in obedience to their professed principle of following the Bible and the Bible only, either to acknowledge this teaching as true, and to return to the observance of ancient Jewish Sabbath, or else to deny that there is any Sabbath at all. And so, in like manner, any one at the present day who should be set about, honestly and without prejudice, to draw up for himself a form of religious belief and practice out of the written word of God, must needs come to the same conclusion: he must either believe that the Jewish Sabbath is still binding upon men's consciences, because of the Divine command, 'Thou shalt keep holy the seventh day;' or he must believe that no Sabbath at all is binding upon them, because of the Apostolic injunction, 'Let no man judge you in respect of a festival day, or of the Sabbaths, which are a shadow of things to come, but the body is Christ's.' Either one or the other of these conclusions he might honestly come to; but he would know nothing whatever of a *Christian* Sabbath distinct from the Jewish, celebrated on a different day, and observed in a different manner, simply because Holy Scripture itself nowhere speaks of such a thing.

"Now, mind in all this you would greatly misunderstand me if you supposed I was quarreling with you for acting in this matter on the true and right principle, in other words, a Catholic principle, viz., the acceptance, without hesitation, of that which has been handed down to you by an unbroken tradition. I would not tear from you a single one of those shreds and fragments of Divine truth which you have retained. God forbid! They are the most precious things you possess, and by God's blessing may serve as clues to bring you out of that labyrinth of error in which you find yourselves involved, far more by the fault of your forefathers three centuries ago than by your own. What do I quarrel with you for is, not your inconsistency in occasionally acting on a true principle, but your adoption, as a general rule, of a false one. You keep the Sunday, and not the Saturday; and you do so rightly, for this was the practice of all Christians when Protestantism began; but you have abandoned other Catholic observances which were equally universal at that day, preferring the novelties introduced by the men who invented Protestantism, to the unvarying tradition of above 1500 years. We blame you not for making Sunday your weekly holyday instead of Saturday, but for rejecting tradition, which is the only safe and clear rule by which this observance can be justified. In outward act we do the same as yourselves in this matter; we too no longer observe the Jewish Sabbath, but Sunday in its stead; but then there is this important difference between us, that we do not pretend, as you do, to derive our authority for so doing from a *book*, but we derive it from a *living teacher*, and that teacher is the Church. Moreover, we believe that not every thing which God would have us to know and to do is written in the Bible, but that is also an unwritten word of God, which we are bound to believe and to obey, just as we believe and obey the Bible itself, according to that saying of the Apostles, 'Stand fast and hold the traditions which you have learned, *whether by word or by our epistle*' (2 Thess. ii 14). We Catholics, then, have precisely the same authority for keeping Sunday holy instead of Saturday as we have for every other article of our creed, namely, the authority of 'the Church of the living God, the pillar and ground of truth' (1 Tim. iii 15); whereas you who are Protestants have really no authority for it whatever; for there *is* no authority for it in the Bible, and you will not allow that there *can be* authority for it anywhere else. Both you and we do, in fact, follow tradition in this matter; but *we* follow it, believing it to be a part of God's word, and the Church to be its divinely-appointed guardian and interpreter; you follow it, denouncing it all the time as a fallible and treacherous guide, which often 'make the commandment of God of none effect.'"

This passage gives five points that Protestants use to justify the Sabbath-to-Sunday change. Keep in mind that this author is a Catholic man. The verses that he presents and with which he gives his explanations are from a Catholic point of view and are not all correct. We examined these verses in an earlier section of this book; however, I will briefly review them to clarify them from a biblical standpoint and not from a denominational viewpoint:

75

1. This author explains Colossians 2:16 by saying, "I could understand a Bible Christian arguing from this passage, that we ought to make no difference between Saturday, Sunday, and every other day of the week." The author, like almost all Christians, thinks that Paul is talking about the weekly Sabbath when he says, "Sabbath-days." Notice that the term is plural. The Hebrews had many Sabbaths, including the annual Sabbath, the seventh-year Sabbath for the planet, and so on. When Paul makes the statement, "Let no one pass judgment on you in questions of food and drink, or with regard to a festival or a new moon, or a Sabbath" (Colossians 2:16), he is referring to the feasts and holy days that were commanded in the Book of the Law written by Moses, and not the weekly Sabbath that is found in the Ten Commandments.

2. The author gives his opinion of Revelation 1:10, which in my opinion is a valid point, but we know that John was present when Jesus said, "I am Lord of the Sabbath"; therefore, we can reason that John was present on the Sabbath, the true Lord's day.

3. He explains 1 Corinthians 16:2 and asks the question: "How is this supposed to affect the law of the Jewish Sabbath?" Notice he calls it the "Jewish Sabbath." Jesus never said the Sabbath was created for the Jews; it was created for all mankind (Mark 2:27).

4. In the fourth point, the author refers to the resurrection of Jesus Christ and the other appearances made by our Lord to His disciples. He then asks, "What is there in these facts to do away with the obligation of keeping holy the seventh day?" This is a valid question, and the answer to which is "nothing."

5. The final point that he makes is the one found in Acts 20:7. Notice that he says, "We have the example of the Apostles themselves." Apostles? Remember that in the previous chapter I covered this verse. Most people believe that when it says "Now on the first day of the week, when the disciples came together to break bread" it refers to the twelve disciples of Jesus, but it actually does not—in fact, it may be that of the twelve apostles, only Luke was present. (For more details, see the section about the apostles and the Sabbath.)

To conclude, this author calls out to Protestants by saying "had someone or other of the 'Reformers' taken it into his head to denounce the observance of Sunday as a Popish corruption and superstition, and to insist upon it that Saturday was the day which God had appointed to be kept holy, and that He had never authorized the observance of any other—all Protestants would have been obliged in obedience to their professed principle of following the Bible and the Bible only." The author's purpose in writing this article is to make Protestants understand that they follow a Catholic tradition by making Sunday a holy day. He said, "We [Catholics] blame you not for making Sunday your weekly holy day instead of Saturday, but for rejecting tradition, which is the only safe and clear rule by which this observance can be justified."

How much more evidence is necessary to prove that the Roman Catholic Church changed the Sabbath from the seventh day of the week to the first day of the week? Friend, I urge you to obey God above man, for the Holy Scriptures say "We must obey God rather than men" (Acts 5:29).

THE LITTLE HORN AND THE BEAST

Now we will examine the mark of the beast as mentioned in the book of Revelation. Many will argue the fact that Sunday is the mark of the beast. However, it is not the day of the week that is the mark, but the spurious Sabbath, also known as the Lord's day. Allow me to explain. To know its mark, we must first identify the beast. In order to do this, we need to study Revelation and Daniel.

In Revelation 13, we first find two beasts—but what does "beast" mean in Bible prophecy? In Daniel 7, the angel tells Daniel that the fourth beast will be a fourth kingdom—in today's terms, a form of government. The angel says, "Thus he said: 'As for the fourth beast, there shall be a fourth kingdom on earth" (Daniel 7:23). Thus, "beast" in biblical prophecy means a kingdom or government.

The first beast from Revelation 13 comes out of the sea, so what does that mean? In Bible prophecy, waters stand for people: "The waters that you saw, where the prostitute is seated, are peoples and multitudes and nations and languages" (Revelation 17:15). But this beast has ten horns and seven heads, with seven diadems on its horns and blasphemous names on its heads.

The first beast from chapter 13 is the same beast that the harlot from chapter17 is riding; therefore, we will need to cover both chapters to better understand the beast and its mark. In chapter 17, we find a harlot riding a beast; since we already know that a beast equals a kingdom or government, we need to determine what the woman means.

According to the Bible, God's church is the bride of God. The Bible says, "For your Maker is your husband . . . For the LORD has called you like a wife deserted and grieved in spirit, like a wife of youth when she is cast off, says your God" (Isaiah 54:5-6). Thus, the harlot is a religious body, a church that has a political identity, which represents the beast. The harlot was arrayed in purple and scarlet, adorned with gold, jewels, and pearls with a golden cup in her hand. On her forehead she had a name—"Babylon the great, mother of prostitutes and of earth's abominations" (Revelation 17:5)—and she was "drunk with the blood of the saints, the blood of the martyrs of Jesus" (verse 6).

So, this harlot is a church that has a political body (the beast); it uses the colors purple and scarlet; it is rich, since she is wearing precious stones (gold, jewels, and pearls); it uses a golden cup (in its services); it is a mother church that has blasphemous names or titles; and it has killed the saints and martyrs of Jesus. The beast has seven heads and ten horns, as the angel tells John: "the seven heads are seven mountains on which the woman is seated; they are also seven kings, five of whom have fallen, one is, the other has not yet come, and when he does come he must remain only a little while" (verses 9-10); "the ten horns that you saw are ten kings who have not yet received royal power" (verse 12). Thus, this political body is going to have seven kings while seated on top of the seven hills; however, in chapter 13, this beast was given authority for 1260 years. The Bible says, "The beast was given a mouth uttering haughty and blasphemous words, and it was allowed to exercise authority for forty-two months" (Revelation 13:5).

Now, how did I come up with 1260 years when the Bible says forty-two months? Well, the Hebrew calendar has thirty days per month, so thirty times forty-two equals 1260 days. A day in Bible prophecy equals a literal year. (See Numbers 14:34 and Ezekiel 4:6)

Just like the harlot from Revelation 17, the beast of chapter 13 had killed the saints: "Also it was allowed to make war on the saints and to conquer them" (Revelation 13:7). The first beast of Revelation chapter 13 has body parts like other animals: "the beast that I saw was like a leopard; its feet were like a bear's, and its mouth was like a lion's mouth" (verse 2). The beast is described this way because as a political body it had traditions that it had copied from past civilizations.

In Daniel 7, Daniel sees four beasts that came out of the water. The first three were a lion, a bear, and a leopard. These kingdoms were Babylon, Medo-Persia, and Greece. Rome was the fourth kingdom, which Daniel saw as a horrible monster that he could not compare to any animal. As the Roman Empire crumbled, it was divided into ten tribes called the Arian or Germanic tribes. These were the Anglo-Saxons, Alemanni, Franks, Visigoths, Suevi, Burgundians, Lombards, Heruli, Vandals, and Ostrogoths. Daniel saw the Roman Empire being divided into ten kingdoms, as described in chapter 7 of his book.

Daniel saw "a fourth beast, terrifying and dreadful and exceedingly strong. It had great iron teeth; it devoured and broke in pieces and stamped what was left with its feet. It was different from all the beasts that were before it, and it had ten horns. I considered the horns, and behold, there came up among them another horn, a little one, before which three of the first horns were plucked up by the roots. And behold, in this horn were eyes like the eyes of a man, and a mouth speaking great things" (Daniel 7:7-8).

The ten horns are the ten Arian or Germanic tribes that Rome was divided into; the one horn that came out and plucked three other horns was a political body that, in order to gain its power, had to take down three of the Arian tribes. The angel tells Daniel the meaning of the fourth beast: "Thus he said: 'As for the fourth beast, there shall be a fourth kingdom on earth, which shall be different from all the kingdoms, and it shall devour the whole earth, and trample it down, and break it to pieces. As for the ten horns, out of this kingdom ten kings shall arise, and another shall arise after them; he shall be different from the former ones, and shall put down three kings. He shall speak words against the Most High, and shall wear out the saints of the Most High, and shall think to change the times and the law; and they shall be given into his hand for a time, times, and half a time" (verses 23-25).

Which king or identity rose out of Rome, destroyed three of the original Arian tribes, spoke words against the Most High, and thought of changing the times and the law of God while the saints were given to its authority for 1260 years? Let's look at Rome's history to tell us exactly who that was. If you are interested in how exactly the Catholic Church destroyed the three Arian tribes, you can read the book *History of the Christian Church* by Wilhelm Moeller and Gustav Kawerau. The book describes each tribe and tells how the Catholic Church destroyed three of them in order to gain its supremacy.

Now, let's turn back to the Bible. The angel tells Daniel that this little horn (papal supremacy) was going to have dominion for time, times, and half a time. The original Aramaic word that Daniel used for time is *iddan iddawn*, which means a year; times is two years and half a time is half a year. Each Hebrew year consists of three hundred and sixty days, so three and half years equals 1260 days. Thus, 1260 prophetic days equals 1260 literal years. The three horns that the papal system uprooted were the Heruli in AD 493, the Vandals in AD 534, and the Ostrogoths in AD 538. Although history tells us that the Ostrogoths were completely destroyed in the year AD 540, history also tells us that the Catholic Church rose to power in the year AD 538, since the Ostrogoth forces were extremely exhausted.

The Catholic Church, with the military help of Justinian, was able to gain power in the year AD 538. In the year AD 533, Justinian created a decree that made the pope the head of all the churches, but it was not until the year AD 538, when Belisarius gave the papal chair to Vigilius, that it began to be enforced. Schaff says, "Vigilius, a pliant creature of Theodora, ascended the papal chair under the military protection of Belisarius" (*History of the Christian Church*, vol. 3, p. 327). Many have denied this, but it is a fact—the Catholic Church rose to its past supremacy in the year AD 538. The Catholic Church is the only organization that fits the characteristics described by Scripture! In the year 1798, exactly 1260 years later, during the French revolution, Pope Pius VI was taken to France as a prisoner, where he died in 1799. This concludes the prophecy of the 1260 years—or time, times, and half a time—found in Daniel 7, or the forty-two months found in the book of Revelation 13.

People may say that I am merely making this prophecy fit the Catholic Church, so I will outline the points or descriptions given by the Bible and then compare them to the Catholic Church to prove that they do in fact describe the Catholic Church.

First, the little horn came out of the fourth beast, which was Rome. The Catholic Church came out of Rome. Second, the Roman Empire was divided into ten Arian or Germanic tribes, and three were uprooted by the little horn. The Catholic Church destroyed three of the tribes in order to gain its past supremacy—the Heruli, Vandals, and Ostrogoths. Third, the Bible says, "He [the little horn] shall speak words against the Most High" (Daniel 7:25). The Catholic Church has spoken against the Most High many times. Let us look at some of their quotes. Pope Pius V said, "The Pope and God are the same, so he [the Pope] has all power in Heaven and earth" ("Cities Petrus Bertanous," in *Barclay*, chap. XXVII, p. 218).

Pope Nicholas said, "I am in all and above all, so that God Himself and I, the vicar of God, hath both one consistory, and I am able to do almost all that God can do... wherefore, if those things that I do be said not to be done of man, but of God, what do you make of me but God? Again, if prelates of the Church be called of Constantine for gods, I then being above all prelates, seem by this reason to be above all gods. Wherefore, no marvel, if it be in my power to dispense with all things, yea with the precepts of Christ" (Decret. par. Distinct 96, chap. 7 edit. Lugo 1661).

"As to papal authority, the Pope is as it were God on earth, sole sovereign of all the faithful of Christ, chief king of kings, having a plentitude of unbroken power, over the earth, with supernatural absolute governing authority entrusted to him by the omnipotent God" (Lucius Ferraris, "Papa," art. 2, in *Prompta Bibliotheca Canonica, Juridica, Moralis, Theologica, Ascetica, Polemica, Rubristica, Historica*, column 1823).

Fourth, the Bible says, "and shall wear out the saints of the Most High," which means to kill the saints. The Catholic Church killed millions of Christians in the Holy Inquisition, which is now known as the doctrine of the faith. This is a well-documented historical era of the church, but I will quote a few authors on this matter. "In one word, the church of Rome has spent immense treasures and shed, in murder, the blood of sixty eight millions and five hundred thousand of the human race, to establish before the astonished and disgusted world, her fixed determination to annihilate every claim set up by the human family to liberty, and the right of unbounded freedom of conscience" (W. C. Brownlee, *Popery the Enemy of Civil and Religious Liberty*, pp. 104-105).

"It has been computed that fifty millions of Protestants have at different times been the victims of the persecutions of the Papists, and put to death for their religious opinions" (Charles Buck, "Persecution," in *A Theological Dictionary*, p. 335).

"That the Church of Rome has shed more innocent blood than any other institution that has ever existed among mankind, will be questioned by no Protestant who has a competent knowledge of history. The memorials, indeed, of many of her persecutions are now so scanty, that it is impossible to form a complete conception of the multitude of her victims, and it is quite certain that no power of imagination can adequately realize their sufferings" (*History of the Rise and Influence of the Spirit of Rationalism in Europe*, vol. 2, p. 32).

There is so much information about the many different persecutions by the Papists; I would need a whole book just for that topic.

Fifth, the next characteristic is that the entity "shall think to change the times and the law [God's Law]." The Roman calendar is the only one we use today, and the tracking of midnight to midnight for a day is not biblical—it comes from Rome. The Bible says that the evening and the morning was a day in Genesis 1. The law of God was changed by the Catholic Church. If you do not believe me, look in the Catholic Catechism for the Ten Commandments and compare it to the Ten Commandments in the Bible, Exodus 20. Did the Catholic Church change the Ten Commandments or not?

Sixth, the next description given by the angel to Daniel was that the entity was going to reign for time, times, and half time, which, as we already established, equals 1260 years. The Papal supremacy lasted from AD 538 to 1798, which equals 1260 years exactly! All the biblical evidence fits perfectly to the Church of Rome and to none other. It is undeniable! Using the beast from Revelation 17, which the harlot is riding and which has seven heads, the angel tells John: "This calls for a mind with wisdom: the seven heads are seven mountains on which the woman is seated; they are also seven kings, five of whom have fallen, one is, the other has not yet come, and when he does come he must remain only a little while" (Revelation 17:9-10).

Vatican City is the throne where the Catholic Church sits. Its location is Rome. Rome is surrounded by seven hills, just like the description given by the angel to John. These hills are even named. They are Aventinus, Palatinus, Capitolinus, Quirinalis, Viminalis, Esquilinus, and Caelius. These are also seven kings per the angel's interpretation. The Catholic Church has been around for a long time, but Vatican City has not! Vatican City came into existence in the year 1929 by the Lateran Treaty. The Encarta encyclopedia says the following: "Vatican City was established in 1929 under terms of the Lateran Treaty, concluded by the Italian government and the papacy after many years of controversy" ("Vatican City," in Microsoft® Encarta® Online Encyclopedia 2009).

"Negotiations for the settlement of the Roman Question began in 1926 between the government of Italy and the Holy See, and in 1929 they culminated in the agreements of the Lateran Treaty, signed for King Victor Emmanuel III of Italy by Prime Minister Benito Mussolini and for Pope Pius XI by Pietro Cardinal Gasparri, papal secretary of state" ("Lateran Treaty," in Microsoft® Encarta® Online Encyclopedia 2009).

Since this treaty there have been seven popes. They are: Pope Pius XI (1922–1939), Pope Pius XII (1939–1958), Pope John XXIII (1958–1963), Pope Paul VI (1963–1978), Pope John Paul (1978, lasted 33days), Pope John Paul II (1978–2005), and Pope Benedict XVI (2005-Present). The Bible prophecy has been fulfilled to the dot.

SABBATH TO SUNDAY CHANGE

The most important point to focus on is that the Catholic Church changed the law of God, especially the fourth commandment, which identifies God as the Creator. The Roman Catholic Church changed the sanctification of the Sabbath to the first day of the week. This is the mark of the beast that is mentioned in the book of Revelation. The spurious Sabbath is the mark of the Catholic Church's authority. It is interesting to note that there are many Catholic officials who have been quoted saying the exact same thing. Following are some quotes to substantiate this claim.

First of all, has the Catholic Church accepted that it changed Sabbath to Sunday worship? A letter was sent to the office of Cardinal Gibbons with regard to the same question: Did the church change the Sabbath to Sunday? Here is the response: "Of course the Catholic Church claims that the change [Saturday Sabbath to Sunday] was her act. . . . And the act is a mark of her ecclesiastical authority in religious things" (H.F. Thomas, Chancellor of Cardinal Gibbons). Notice that he says, "a mark of her ecclesiastical authority."

Another Catholic official said: "It was the Catholic church which . . . has transferred this rest to Sunday in remembrance of the resurrection of our Lord. Therefore the observance of Sunday by the Protestants is an homage they pay, in spite of themselves, to the authority of the [Catholic] church" (Monsignor Louis Segur, *Plain Talk About the Protestantism of Today*, p. 213). He also mentions the church's authority, a mark, just like the Bible says.

There is much more evidence. Here is another quote: "They [the Protestants] deem it their duty to keep the Sunday holy. Why? Because the Catholic Church tells them to do so, they have no other reason. . . . The observance of Sunday thus comes to be an ecclesiastical law entirely distinct from the divine law of Sabbath observance. . . .

The author of the Sunday law. . . is the Catholic Church" (*American Ecclesiastical Review*, February 1914).

"For example, nowhere in the Bible do we find that Christ or the Apostles ordered that the Sabbath be changed from Saturday to Sunday. We have the commandment of God given to Moses to keep holy the Sabbath day, that is the 7th day of the week, Saturday. Today most Christians keep Sunday because it has been revealed to us by the [Roman Catholic] church outside the Bible" ("To Tell You the Truth," *Catholic Virginian*, October 3, 1947, p. 9).

Peter R. Kraemer made the following declaration regarding Protestants who allegedly follow the Bible and yet do not keep the Sabbath. During a meeting of the Catholic Church Extension Society in Chicago, Illinois, in 1975, he said,

> "Regarding the change from the observance of the Jewish Sabbath to the Christian Sunday, I wish to draw your attention to the facts:
> 1) That Protestants, who accept the Bible as the only rule of faith and religion, should by all means go back to the observance of the Sabbath. The fact that they do not, but on the contrary observe the Sunday, stultifies them in the eyes of every thinking man.
> 2) We Catholics do not accept the Bible as the only rule of faith. Besides the Bible we have the living Church, the authority of the Church, as a rule to guide us. We say, this Church, instituted by Christ to teach and guide man through life, has the right to change the ceremonial laws of the Old Testament and hence, we accept her change of the Sabbath to Sunday. We frankly say, yes, the Church made this change, made this law, as she made many other laws, for instance, the Friday abstinence, the unmarried priesthood, the laws concerning mixed marriages, the regulation of Catholic marriages and a thousand other laws."

The Catholic Church has always accused Protestants of not following the Bible, and for good reason, most do not! A Catholic priest, Rev. Stephen Keenan, in a question-and-answer section in his book *A Doctrinal Catechism* declared the following:

> Q. Have you any other proofs that they [Protestants] are not guided by the Scripture?
>
> A. Yes; so many, that we cannot admit more than a mere specimen into this small work. They reject much that is clearly contained in Scripture, and profess more that is nowhere discovererable in that Divine Book.

> Q. Give some examples of both?
>
> A. They should, if the Scripture were their only rule, wash the feet of one another, according to the command of Christ. In the 13th chap. of St. John; they should keep, not Sunday but the Saturday, according to the commandment, 'Remember thou keep holy the SABBATH-day;' for this commandment has not in Scripture, been changed or abrogated.

> Q. Has the Church any right to appoint feast days?
>
> A. The Christian Church has surely a right, which even the Jewish Church possessed.

> Q. Where do you find, in the Old Testament feasts of precept instituted by the synagogue?
>
> A. In the Book of Esther, chap 9th, and in the last chapter of the Book of Judith.

> Q. Have you any other way of proving that the Church has power to institute festivals of precept?
>
> A. Had she not such power, she could not have done that in which all modern religionists agree with her; she could not have substituted the observance of Sunday the first day of the week, for the observance of Saturday the seventh day, a change for which there is no Scriptural authority (pp. 100-101, 174).

The Catholic Church claims authority over everything—even over God, which is blasphemy!

Sabbath to Sunday From a Protestant's View

Let us read some of the things the Protestants have said regarding Sunday sabbath observance.

"And where are we told in the Scriptures that we are to keep the first day at all? We are commanded to keep the seventh; but we are nowhere commanded to keep the first day. . . . The reason why we keep the first day of the week holy instead of the seventh is for the same reason that we observe many other things, not because the Bible, but because the church has enjoined it" (Isaac Williams, *Plain Sermons on the Catechism*, vol. 1, pp. 334, 336). This gentleman is honest by accepting the fact that "the Church [Catholic] has enjoined it" when many other preachers deny this fact and still believe that there is a doctrine found in Scriptures, but there isn't.

"The Christian Sabbath is not in the Scriptures, and was not by the primitive church, called the Sabbath" (Timothy Dwight, *Theology: Explained & Defended*, sermon 107, 1818 ed., vol. IV, p. 41). This gentleman says, "the Christian Sabbath" because most Christians believe the Sabbath was for the Jews and Sunday is the Christian Sabbath. However, he admits that the Scriptures do not refer to Sunday as a day of worship. The seventh day is the Sabbath for all humanity: Greek or Jew.

"It is quite clear that however rigidly or devoted we may spend Sunday, we are not keeping the Sabbath. . . . The Sabbath was founded on a specific Divine command. We can plead no such command for the obligation to observe Sunday. . . . There is not a single sentence in the New Testament to suggest that we incur any penalty by violating the supposed sanctity of Sunday" (R. W. Dale, *The Ten Commandments*, pp. 100-101).

No matter how much you think you are keeping the Sabbath on the first day of the week it is not going to change the fact that the Sabbath is the seventh day, which is clearly stated by God in the fourth commandment. If you are not keeping the Sabbath, you are violating the law of God, which is sin according to Scripture. The Bible says, "Whosoever committeth sin transgresseth also the law: for sin is the transgression of the law" (1 John 3:4, KJV). That is the main point: sin is the violation of the law of God. Sinners will not enter the kingdom of heaven. The Bible says: "And there shall in no wise enter into it any thing that defileth, neither whatsoever worketh abomination, or maketh a lie: but they which are written in the Lamb's book of life" (Revelation 21:27, KJV).

THE CLAIMED AUTHORITY OF THE ROMAN CHURCH

The following section was taken from the book *A Protestant's Appeal to the Douay Bible*, which was written by Rev. John Jenkins. The author quotes a Roman Catholic work, "Ferraris Bibliotheca Prompta," which is an authorized standard of Roman Catholic divinity. The extract may be found in the Frankfort edition, which was printed in 1783, under the word "Papa."

"The Pope is of such dignity and highness, that he is not simply a man, but as it were, God, and the Vicar of God. Hence the Pope is of such supreme and sovereign dignity that, properly speaking, he is not merely constituted in dignity, but is rather placed on the very summit of dignities. Hence also the Pope is 'Father of Fathers;' and he alone can use this name, because he only can be called 'Father of Fathers,' since he possesses the primacy over all, is truly greater than all, and the greatest of all. He is called 'most holy,' because he is presumed to be such. On account of the Excellency of his supreme dignity, he is called 'Bishop of Bishops, Ordinary of Ordinaries, universal Bishop of the Church, Bishop or Diocesan of the whole world, divine Monarch, supreme Emperor and King of Kings.' Hence the Pope is crowned with a triple crown, as King of heaven, of earth, and of hell. Nay, the Pope's excellence and power is not only about heavenly, terrestrial and infernal things, but he is also above angels, and is their superior; so that if it were possible that angels could err from the faith, or entertain sentiments contrary thereto, they could be judged and excommunicated by the Pope. He is of such great tribunal and power, that he occupies one and the same tribunal with Christ; so that whatsoever the Pope does, seems to proceed from the mouth of God, as is proved from many Doctors. The Pope is as it were God on earth, the only Prince of the faithful of Christ, the greatest King of Kings, possessing the plentitude of power, to whom the government of the earthly and heavenly kingdom is entrusted" (pp. 75-76).

The following quotes were extracted from *The American Quarterly Church Review and Ecclesiastical Register*:

"Thomas Aquinas says: — 'In the Pope is the summit of power. When any one is denounced excommunicated by his decision on account of apostasy his subjects are immediately freed from his dominion and their oath of allegiance to him. The Pope by divine right hath spiritual and temporal power as supreme king of the world so that he can impose taxes on all Christians and destroy towns and castles for the preservation of Christianity.'

"Benedict XIV in his work on Synodical Affairs says: — 'The Pope is head of all heads and the prince moderator and pastor of the whole Church of Christ under heaven.'

"In the preface of a work on Ecclesiastical Power dedicated to Pope John XXII and extracted by Power Barrow writes: — 'It is an error not to believe that the Roman Pontiff is pastor of the universal Church the successor of Peter the vicar of Christ and that he hath not universal supremacy over temporal and spiritual matters'" (vol. 21, pp. 166-167).

By this claimed authority, the Roman Catholic Church changed Sabbath to Sunday. During the Council of Trent, the Roman Catholic Church responded to the Protestant's Reformation about crucial doctrinal points, defining the church's teachings in the areas of Scripture and tradition. One of the responses of the Roman Catholic Church was that the church's authority was above Scripture.[1]

---

1   Gaspar de Fosso, the Archbishop of Reggio: "Die Autorität der Kirche könne fchon deßhalb nicht gebunden fein an die Autorität der Schrift weil jene nicht nach der Anordnung Christi sondern aus eigener Autorität die Beschneidung in die Taufe den Sabbat in den Sonntag verwandelt habe."

Translated to English: "The authority of the church could therefore not be bound to the authority of the Scriptures, because the church had changed circumcision into baptism, Sabbath into Sunday, not by the command of Christ, but by its own authority" (Heinrich Julius Holtzmann, *Kanon und Tradition*, p. 263).

Dear reader, Sunday observance has no biblical evidence; it is a law of the Roman Catholic Church. Do you want to obey God and keep His law, or do you want to obey the beast and receive its mark? It is your decision, but remember, the Bible says, "And another angel, a third, followed them, saying with a loud voice, 'If anyone worships the beast and its image and receives a mark on his forehead or on his hand, he also will drink the wine of God's wrath, poured full strength into the cup of his anger, and he will be tormented with fire and sulfur in the presence of the holy angels and in the presence of the Lamb. And the smoke of their torment goes up forever and ever, and they have no rest, day or night, these worshipers of the beast and its image, and whoever receives the mark of its name" (Revelation 14:9-11).

THE LATTER SUNDAY LAW

The Bible says, "Also it causes all, both small and great, both rich and poor, both free and slave, to be marked on the right hand or the forehead" (Revelation 13:16). This is not a literal mark as some Christians teach, because if it was, God's seal would have to be literal as well. I already identified the mark of the beast to be the false Sabbath, which is Sunday. There is coming a time when laws will be instituted in the United States making Sunday holy. If you do not believe in God but are a law-abiding citizen, you will follow this law, which means that you will receive "the mark of the beast" on your right hand in God's eyes. If you do believe that Sunday is the new Christian Sabbath, replacing the true Sabbath given by God, you will receive it on your forehead (representing your mind and beliefs).

There are already laws in the United States that make Sunday a day of rest; these are known as the "blue laws." These laws are not national yet, so it is not the fulfillment of the prophecy. However, soon, in the United States of America, laws will be passed to honor Sunday as a holy day. The separation between church and state will be no more, and the church will use the state's authority to implement the Sunday doctrine by law. With the blue laws present in many states, it is not too difficult to imagine a day when the entire nation will be required to worship on Sunday.

Morality in the country is at an all time low. Because of the current state of affairs, what better way is there to increase morality than to keep the Lord's day and have people go to church. Sounds good? By forcing the conscience of the masses into accepting the spurious sabbath, the mark of the beast will be placed on those who worship on Sunday, and those that accept it will be sealed for perdition.

The Bible gives a warning to mankind not to accept this mark. It says, "And another angel, a third, followed them, saying with a loud voice, 'If anyone worships the beast and its image and receives a mark on his forehead or on his hand, he also will drink the wine of God's wrath, poured full strength into the cup of his anger, and he will be tormented with fire and sulfur in the presence of the holy angels and in the presence of the Lamb" (Revelation 14:9–10). By keeping Sunday holy, individuals are worshipping the papists (the beast), and the image of the beast are those Protestant churches, daughters of the whore from Revelation 17, that teach man to keep Sunday holy, thus creating an image of their mother church.

Dear reader, the Bible urges you to worship the Creator of heaven and earth: "Worship him who made heaven and earth, the sea and the springs of water" (Revelation 14:7). The Sabbath commandment identifies Jehovah as the Creator: "For in six days the LORD[1] made heaven and earth, the sea, and all that in them is, and rested on the seventh day. Therefore the LORD blessed the Sabbath day and made it holy" (Exodus 20:11).

The Catholic Church believes that if you keep Sunday holy you are worshipping the pope and the church (the beast). "It was the Catholic church which . . . has transferred this rest to Sunday in remembrance of the resurrection of our Lord. Therefore the observance of Sunday by the Protestants is an homage they pay, in spite of themselves, to the authority of the [Catholic] church" (Monsignor Louis Segur, *Plain Talk About the Protestantism of Today*, p. 213).

Do you want to worship the beast, or do you want to worship Him who created the heavens and the earth? Remember the angel's warning to those who receive the mark and the consequences that they will suffer—the wrath of God displayed in the seven plagues described in Revelation 16.

---

1   Strong's Hebrew and Greek dictionary— "yehôvâh; yeh-ho-vaw"; From H1961; (the) self Existent or eternal; Jehovah, Jewish national name of God: — Jehovah, the Lord." Compare H3050, H3069.

There is a group of men and women who tells the beast: "We will not serve your god, we will not bow down before your image. Jehovah is our King!" Do you want to be a part of this group?

We'd love to have you download our
catalog of titles we publish at:

www.TEACHServices.com

or write or email us your thoughts,
reactions, or criticism about this
or any other book we publish at:

TEACH Services, Inc.
254 Donovan Road
Brushton, New York 12916

info@TEACHServices.com

or you may call us at:
518/358-3494

www.ingramcontent.com/pod-product-compliance
Lightning Source LLC
Chambersburg PA
CBHW060551100426
42742CB00013B/2518

* 9 7 8 1 5 7 2 5 8 6 1 8 5 *